JOB

Trusting God in Suffering

John MacArthur

THOMAS NELSON

Since 1798

MacArthur Bible Studies
Job: Trusting God in Suffering
© 2020 by John MacArthur

Published in Nashville, Tennessee, by Thomas Nelson. Thomas Nelson is a registered trademark of HarperCollins Christian Publishing, Inc.

"Unleashing God's Truth, One Verse at a Time ®" is a trademark of Grace to You. All rights reserved.

All Scripture quotations are taken from The Holy Bible, New King James Version. Copyright © 1979, 1980, 1982 by Thomas Nelson. All rights reserved.

Some material from the Introduction, "Keys to the Text" and "Exploring the Meaning" sections are taken from *The MacArthur Bible Commentary*, John MacArthur. Copyright © 2005 Thomas Nelson Publishers.

Thomas Nelson titles may be purchased in bulk for educational, business, fundraising, or sales promotional use. For information, please e-mail SpecialMarkets@ThomasNelson.com.

ISBN 978-0-310-11628-8 (softcover)
ISBN 978-0-310-12377-4 (ebook)

First Printing September 2020 / Printed in the United States of America

HB 05.21.2024

CONTENTS

INTRODUCTION

Why does suffering exist in the world? Why does God allow the righteous to endure tragedy when the wicked often seem to enjoy lives of luxury? Where is God in time of pain? These questions have puzzled people for centuries, with no easy answers at hand. Thankfully, we can wrestle with the underlying themes of those questions by exploring the story of Job.

In these twelve studies, we will examine the events in the book of Job. We will witness the curtain being pulled back on the supernatural forces at work in our world and see Satan's role as the agitator behind some of the pain and suffering we experience. We will read how Job had everything stripped away in a single day—his children, servants, wealth, and health—and how this forced him to grapple with the reality of suffering. We will meet Job's four "friends" and hear how they pushed Job to accept the belief that suffering is always a punishment for sin and rebellion against God. Ultimately, we will see God intervene in the debate, teaching Job and his friends a valuable lesson about His sovereignty.

Through it all, we will learn why it is appropriate to cry out to God in the midst of our tragedy—and even express our anguish and our desire for relief. In the end, we will discover, as Job came to realize, that God is sovereign, infinitely wise, loving, and full of compassion, so we must trust Him in every situation—even when those attributes seem to be eclipsed for a time.

TITLE

The book of Job bears the name of the narrative's primary character. This name might have been derived from the Hebrew word for *persecution* (meaning "persecuted one" or from an Arabic word meaning *repent* (thus "repentant one"). The author recounts an era in the life of Job, in which he was tested and the character of God was revealed. Paul quoted from Job (see Romans 11:35 and 1 Corinthians 3:19), and James referred to him as well (see James 5:11).

AUTHOR

The book does not name its author. Job is an unlikely candidate, as the book's message rests on his ignorance of the events in heaven that related to his ordeal. One tradition suggests that Moses was the author, for the land of Midian where he lived for forty years was adjacent to Uz (see 1:1), and he could have obtained a record of the story there. Solomon is also a possibility, due to the similarity of content with parts of Ecclesiastes and the other wisdom books. Elihu, Isaiah, Hezekiah, Jeremiah, and Ezra have also been suggested as authors, but without support.

DATE

It is likely that the book of Job was written much later than the events depicted in its pages. Job had a lifespan of nearly 200 years (see 42:16), which fits the patriarchal period (e.g., Abraham lived 175 years according to Genesis 25:7). Furthermore, the social unit was structured around the patriarchal family, the Chaldeans (who murdered Job's servants) were still nomadic and not yet city dwellers (see 1:17), Job's wealth was measured in livestock rather than gold and silver (see 1:3; 42:12), Job conducted priestly functions within his family (see 1:4–5), and the text is silent on matters such as the covenant of Abraham, Israel, the Exodus, and the Law of Moses. However, Job appears to know about Adam (see 31:33) and the flood (see 12:15). These features appear to place the events chronologically at a time after the Tower of Babel (see Genesis 11:1–9) but before or contemporaneous with Abraham (see Genesis 11:27).

BACKGROUND AND SETTING

This book begins with a scene in heaven that explains to the reader everything that will take place (see 1:6–2:10). Job was suffering because God was contesting with Satan. Job did not know this, nor did his friends; so they all struggled to explain suffering from the perspective of their ignorance. Finally, Job rested in nothing but his faith in God's goodness and the hope of His redemption, and his trust was then vindicated by God's intervention and the full restoration of Job.

The overall message of the book is to trust God even when there seem to be no rational, or even theological, explanations for disaster, pain, and suffering.

HISTORICAL AND THEOLOGICAL THEMES

The events that occur in the book of Job present readers with a profound question: "Why do the righteous suffer?" Although an answer to this question seems important, the book does not set forth such a response. Job never learned the reasons for his suffering. In fact, when God finally confronted Job, he could only put his hand over his mouth and say nothing. His silence underscores the importance of trusting God's purposes in the midst of suffering, because suffering—like all other human experiences—is directed by perfect divine wisdom.

The book treats two major themes, both in the narrative framework of the prologue (see Job 1–2) and epilogue (see 42:7–17), and in the poetic account of Job's torment that lies in between (see 3:1–42:6). A key to understanding the first theme is to notice the debate between God and Satan in heaven and how it connects with the three cycles of earthly debates between Job and his friends. God wanted to prove the character of believers to Satan and all demons, angels, and people. Satan had objected that God's claims of Job's righteousness were untested. He accused the righteous of being faithful to God only for what they could get in return.

Satan's confidence that he could turn Job against God came, no doubt, from the fact that he had led the holy angels to rebel with him. Satan thought he could destroy Job's faith by inflicting suffering on him. God released Satan to make his point. But Satan failed, as Job's true faith in God proved unbreakable. Satan tried to do the same to Peter (see Luke 22:31–34) and was unsuccessful in destroying his faith (see John 21:15–19). In the end, God proved that saving faith can't be destroyed, no matter how much trouble a saint endures.

A second theme concerns the character of God to humans. Does this ordeal between God and Satan, with Job as the test case, suggest that God is lacking in mercy? Not at all. James writes, "You have heard of the perseverance of Job and seen the end intended by the Lord—that the Lord is very compassionate and merciful" (James 5:11). God wanted Job to ultimately benefit through the ordeal by learning to trust in Him as the sovereign and perfectly wise Creator. In the end, we find that God floods Job with more blessings than he had ever known.

The book opens with a declaration that Job was "blameless and upright, and one who feared God and shunned evil" (1:1)—and then addresses the inscrutable mystery of why such people suffer. God ordains that His children walk in sorrow and pain, sometimes because of sin, sometimes for chastening, sometimes for strengthening, and sometimes to give opportunity to reveal His comfort and grace. But there are times when the issue in the suffering is unknowable because it is for a heavenly purpose that those on earth can't discern.

By spreading out the elements of this great theme, we can see the following truths in Job's experience. First, there are matters going on in heaven we know nothing about, yet those matters affect our lives. Second, even the best effort at explaining the issues of life can be useless. Third, bad things happen all the time to good people, so we cannot judge a person's spirituality by circumstances. Fourth, God is always good, and we can safely leave our lives in His hands. Fifth, we should not abandon God in suffering but draw near to Him, so that out of the fellowship can come the comfort. Sixth, the suffering may be intense, but it will ultimately end for the righteous—and God will bless them abundantly.

INTERPRETIVE CHALLENGES

The most critical interpretive challenge involves the book's primary message. The answer to why Job suffers is never directly revealed to him, though the reader knows that it involves God proving a certain point to Satan. Readers find themselves putting their proverbial hands over their mouths, with no right to question or accuse the all-wise and all-powerful Creator, who will do as He pleases. Engaging in "theodicy" (attempting to defend God's involvement in calamity) is shown to be appropriate in these circumstances. However, in the end, it is apparent that God does not need or want a human advocate.

The nature of Job's guilt and innocence raises perplexing questions. God declares Job perfect and upright (see 1:1). But Job's comforters, based on his ordeal, question whether he is secretly harboring some scandalous sin. On several occasions, Job readily admits to having sinned (see 7:21; 13:26), but he questions the extent of his sin as compared to the severity of his suffering. God eventually rebukes Job for his demands to be vindicated of the comforters' accusations. But He also declares that what Job said was correct and what the comforters said was wrong.

Another challenge comes in understanding the viewpoints that Job and his comforters brought into the ordeal. At the outset, all agreed that God punishes evil, rewards obedience, and does so without exception. But Job, due to his suffering innocently, was forced to conclude that exceptions are possible in that the righteous also suffer. He also observed that the wicked prosper. These are more than small exceptions to the rule, thus forcing Job to rethink his simple understanding about God's sovereign interaction with His people. The type of wisdom Job comes to embrace was not dependent merely on the promise of reward or punishment.

The long, peevish disputes between Job and his accusers serve as attempts to reconcile the perceived inequities of God's retribution in Job's experiences. Such an empirical method is dangerous. In the end, God offers no explanation to Job, but He calls all parties to a deeper level of trust in the Creator, who rules over a sin-confused world with power and authority, as directed by His perfect wisdom and mercy.

Understanding the book thus requires (1) understanding the nature of wisdom, particularly the difference between man's and God's, and (2) admitting that Job and his friends lacked the divine wisdom needed to interpret Job's circumstances accurately. The resolution of this matter is found in Job 28, where the character of divine wisdom is explained. Divine wisdom is rare and priceless, we cannot hope to purchase it, and God possesses it all. We may not always know God's purposes on earth, but we must trust Him. Because of this, the matter of believers' suffering takes a back seat to the matter of divine wisdom.

1

THE DILEMMA

Job 1:1–3:1

DRAWING NEAR
How do you typically respond when you face tragedy or loss?

_____

_____

_____

_____

_____

_____

_____

_____

_____

_____

_____

_____

THE CONTEXT
Job likely lived during the same era as Abraham and the other patriarchs listed in the book of Genesis. Job was a servant of God during a time when the Lord had not yet revealed His law to Moses or established the sacrificial system for seeking atonement. Nevertheless, Job had a personal relationship with God, which he expressed through a rhythm of worship and sacrifice.

Job himself is introduced as someone who has achieved the pinnacle of success in life. He is a man of integrity, "blameless and upright," who fears God and shuns evil (1:1). He has been blessed with a large family, including sons and daughters. He has many servants and is a person of means, with flocks of sheep, camels, oxen, and donkeys—a notable achievement in an agrarian society with no established currency. In short, Job has it all.

The early chapters of Job contain most of the action in the book, beginning with Satan's accusation to God that Job would not remain spiritually faithful if his material blessings were removed. God allows Satan to strike all that Job values through a series of calamities, which results in Job losing all his children, servants, and wealth. Later, God allows Satan to strike at Job's health through painful boils all over his body. This narrative section ends when Job's three friends come to offer comfort because "they saw that his grief was very great" (2:13).

KEYS TO THE TEXT

Read Job 1:1–3:1, noting the key words and phrases indicated below.

> JOB AND HIS FAMILY: *Job is introduced as a man with spiritual integrity and material wealth. He has a large family and is considered one of the greatest in his day.*

1:1. Uz: Job's home was a walled city with gates, and there he had earned a position of great respect (see 29:7–8). The city was in the land of Uz in northern Arabia, adjacent to Midian, where Moses had lived for forty years (see Exodus 2:15).

BLAMELESS AND UPRIGHT: Job was not perfect or without sin (see, for example, 6:24; 7:21; 9:20). However, he had put his trust in God for redemption and had faithfully lived a God-honoring and sincere life of integrity—both personally, maritally, and parentally.

3. HIS POSSESSIONS WERE SEVEN THOUSAND SHEEP: Job's wealth, as was typical in the ancient Near East, was not measured in money or land holdings but in his numerous livestock. He was similar to the patriarch Abraham, who "was very rich in livestock" (Genesis 13:2).

GREATEST OF ALL THE PEOPLE OF THE EAST: This is a major claim by any standard. Solomon gained a similar reputation: "Solomon's wisdom excelled the wisdom of all the men of the East" (1 Kings 4:30). The "East" denotes those people living east of the land of Palestine.

4. ON HIS APPOINTED DAY: Each of the seven sons had an appointed day of the week. This reference to the main meal of each day of the week, which moved from house to house, implies the love and harmony of the family members. The sisters are especially noted to show these were cared for with love.

5. SEND AND SANCTIFY: At the end of every week, Job would offer up as many burnt offerings as he had sons (see Leviticus 1:4), officiating weekly as the family priest. These offerings were to cover any sin that his children may have committed that week, indicating the depth of his spiritual devotion. This record is included to demonstrate the righteousness and virtue of Job and his family, which made his suffering all the more amazing.

BURNT OFFERINGS: This kind of offering was known as early as Noah. "Then Noah built an altar to the LORD, and took of every clean animal and of every clean bird, and offered burnt offerings on the altar" (Genesis 8:20).

THE CURTAIN IS PULLED BACK: *In the throne room of heaven, Satan attacks Job's character, claiming he is only faithful to God because of his blessings.*

6. SONS OF GOD: Job's life is about to be caught up in heavenly strategies as the scene moves from earth to heaven, where God is holding council with His court. It is significant to note that neither Job nor his friends ever come to know about these events. All of their discussions are conducted without the benefit of knowing about this heavenly dimension.

SATAN: As a title means "adversary," used in either a personal or judicial sense. This arch-demon is the ultimate spiritual adversary of all time and has been accusing the righteous throughout the ages (see Revelation 12:10). In a courtroom setting, the adversary usually stood to the right of the accused. In Zechariah 3:1, we find Satan in this place when he accused Joshua the High Priest. Paul's thesis in Romans 8:31–39 is that Satan remains unsuccessful in his attempts to accuse the faithful servants of God.

7. AND THE LORD SAID: Lest there be any question about God's role in this ordeal, it was He who initiated the dialogue. The adversary was not presiding. If anything, Satan raised the penetrating question that might well be asked by anyone, perhaps even Job himself: "Does Job serve God with pure motives,

3

or is he in it only as long as the blessings flow?" Spiritually speaking, is Job merely a "fair weather" believer in God?

GOING TO AND FRO ON THE EARTH: The picture is of haste. No angel, fallen or holy, is an omnipresent creature, but they move rapidly. In Satan's case, as prince of this world (see John 12:31; 14:30; 16:11) and ruler of demons (see Matthew 9:34; 12:24), the earth is where he prowls like a "roaring lion, seeking whom he may devour" (1 Peter 5:8).

12. IN YOUR POWER: God allows Satan to test Job's faith by attacking "all that he has." God sovereignly allows Satan to move against Job—except that he cannot attack him physically.

> ATTACK: *Satan begins to demonstrate his power on earth, with the result that Job is soon stripped of everything that he values in life.*

13: NOW THERE WAS A DAY: With four rapid-fire disasters, Satan destroys or removes Job's livestock, servants, and children. Only the four messengers survive.

15. SABEANS: Literally "Sheba," part of Arabia. These people were terrorizing robbers who had descended from Ham and/or Shem (see Genesis 10:6–7; 10:21, 28).

16. FIRE OF GOD . . . HEAVEN: This likely refers to severe lightning.

17. CHALDEANS: A semi-nomadic people of the Arabian desert who were experienced in marauding and war (see, for example, Habakkuk 1:6–8).

19. GREAT WIND: This likely refers to a tornado-type wind (see Isaiah 21:1; Hosea 13:15).

20. FELL TO THE GROUND AND WORSHIPED: Job remains calm when he learns of all his losses, but he expresses extreme grief when he learns of the death of his children. However, instead of cursing God, he chooses to bless the name of the Lord. Job's submissive response disproves Satan's accusations. So far, Job has proved to be what God claimed him to be.

22. DID NOT SIN NOR CHARGE GOD WITH WRONG: This is better rendered, "did not sin by charging God with wrong." Hasty words against God in the midst of grief are foolish and wicked. Christians are to submit to trials and still worship God, not because they see the reasons for the trials, but because they trust that God has His own reasons for them (see 2 Corinthians 4:7–18).

ANOTHER LAYER: Satan's initial attack is unsuccessful, and God again points out the example of his faithfulness. But Satan insists that Job will crumble if he suffers physical harm. God allows it but prevents Satan from taking Job's life.

2:3. STILL HE HOLDS FAST TO HIS INTEGRITY: God affirms that Job has won round one.

WITHOUT CAUSE: This is a crucial statement. When Job's friends later try to explain why the disasters have befallen him, they always put the blame on Job. Grasping this truth that God is not punishing Job for something he has done is crucial to understanding the message of Job. Sometimes, suffering is caused by divine purposes that are unknowable to us.

4. SKIN FOR SKIN: Satan contends that what he has done to Job so far is just "scratching the surface." Job has endured the loss of all he had, even the lives of his children, but will not endure the loss of his own wellbeing. Satan contends that if God allows him to make the disaster a personal matter of Job's own physical body, his faith will fail.

6. SPARE HIS LIFE: The Lord agrees but sovereignly limits Satan's ability to cause harm. However, for Job, the torment makes death seem preferable (see 7:15).

8. HE SAT IN THE MIDST OF THE ASHES: Job takes himself to where the lepers went: the ash heap outside the city. There he scrapes at his sores with a piece of broken pottery, perhaps breaking them open to release the pressure and infection.

9. YOUR INTEGRITY: But Job's faith remains, so that his wife cannot accuse him of insincerity, as Satan had. Her argument, in effect, is for Job to let go of his piety and curse God, and then the Almighty will end Job's life for his blasphemy. (In other words, death under those conditions would be preferable to living.) She basically advises Job to sin!

11. TEMANITE: Most likely, Teman was a city of Edom (see Genesis 36:4, 11).

SHUHITE: Descendants of Abraham through Keturah (see Genesis 25:2, 6).

NAAMATHITE: A resident of an unknown location probably in Edom or Arabia, though some have suggested Naamah on the Edomite border (see Joshua 15:41).

13. HIS GRIEF WAS VERY GREAT: The expression actually meant that Job's disease produced pain that was increasing. The agony was so great that his friends were speechless for a week.

3:1 CURSED THE DAY OF HIS BIRTH. Job is in deep despair, and while he does not curse God, he does curse the day of his birth. Job wishes that he had never been born, because not even the joys he had previously experienced in his life were worth all this pain.

UNLEASHING THE TEXT

1) What were some of the blessings that Job enjoyed at the beginning of his story?

_____

_____

_____

_____

2) What do these chapters in Job reveal about Satan's character, nature, and power?

_____

_____

_____

_____

_____

3) How would you summarize or describe God's role in these chapters?

_____

_____

_____

_____

_____

4) In what ways did Job respond well after he lost everything he valued?

_____

_____

_____

_____

_____

EXPLORING THE MEANING

God knows His children. One truth that stands out from Job is that God is fully aware of our lives. He sees us and knows our actions, our conversations, and even our thoughts. There is nothing that escapes His attention and nothing about us He does not comprehend.

What an amazing truth! God is the Creator of everything that exists—worlds upon worlds, galaxies upon galaxies, and more. Not only that, but God sustains all that exists. Were God to remove Himself from creation at any point, everything we know would crumble and fade—just like the picture on your TV winks out as soon as you unplug the power cord.

Yet in spite of everything that requires God's attention, He still has the capacity and the interest to follow the details of a single human life such as Job's. God even pointed Job out to Satan, noting that he was "a blameless and upright man, one who fears God and shuns evil" (1:8). God knew Job intimately. He knows each of us intimately as well.

God allows the suffering of His children. Another truth that cannot be avoided is that God, in His sovereignty, will sometimes allow His children to endure suffering. It was God who brought Job to Satan's attention. When Satan then scoffed that Job's righteousness was only a byproduct of God's blessings, the Lord allowed Satan to remove those blessings. "Behold, all that he has is in your power; only do not lay a hand on his person" (1:12).

The tragedy Job experienced was horrifying. He lost his children, his servants, and his wealth—all in a single day. Yet the Bible says, "In all this Job did not sin nor charge God with wrong" (verse 22). Even so, Satan once again spurned Job's integrity, claiming to God that Job would respond differently if he lost his health as well. Once again, God allowed Satan's attack: "And the LORD said to Satan, 'Behold, he is in your hand, but spare his life'" (2:6).

It is clear that God could have prevented Job's suffering, yet He chose not to do so. He allowed Satan to attack, knowing that Job would undergo great harm. The same is true of God's children today. He is aware of everything we experience, including all the ways we have suffered hurt, heartache, humiliation, and more. God could have prevented each of those incidents, yet He chose to allow them.

Of course, the question that comes immediately to mind is, "Why?" Why would God allow any person to suffer? We will engage that question several times throughout this study, because it remains a central theme throughout the book of Job.

God is more powerful than His enemies. Even when we don't understand the "why?" of suffering, we can take solace in the truth that God is more powerful than Satan. Notice the limits that God placed on the attacks leveled by Satan against Job: "And the LORD said to Satan, 'Behold, all that he has is in your power; only do not lay a hand on his person'" (1:12). "And the LORD said to Satan, 'Behold, he is in your hand, but spare his life'" (2:6).

God commanded Satan, and Satan had no choice but to obey His command. This may seem surprising at first, because we know that Satan is God's fiercest and most determined enemy. His entire existence is defined by rebellion against God and everything that God represents. In describing Satan, Jesus said, "He was a murderer from the beginning, and does not stand in the truth, because there is no truth in him. When he speaks a lie, he speaks from his own resources, for he is a liar and the father of it" (John 8:44).

Yet in spite of all Satan's evil and all his malice, he could not resist God's command. This is because God is ultimately sovereign and greater than His enemies.

REFLECTING ON THE TEXT

5) Do you find it comforting or frightening that God knows everything about you? Explain.

_____

_____

_____

_____

_____

6) Why is it important for you to understand that God must allow all the suffering you will experience throughout your life?

_____

_____

_____

_____

_____

7) What is your current answer to the question, "Why does God allow suffering in this world?" How has that answer changed over the course of your life?

_____

_____

_____

_____

_____

8) Where do you see evidence in the world today that God is more powerful than any who stand against Him?

_____

_____

_____

_____

_____

PERSONAL RESPONSE

9) What steps will you take to imitate Job in your prayer life this week?

_____

_____

_____

_____

10) How can you prepare yourself now for the reality of suffering so that you will know how to respond when you experience it in the future?

_____

_____

_____

_____

_____

2

AN ACCUSATION OF SIN
Job 4:1–6:30; 8:1–9:35

DRAWING NEAR
Where do you usually go when you need some helpful advice? Why do you
go to that person?

_____

_____

_____

_____

_____

_____

THE CONTEXT
In the previous study, we saw how three of Job's friends appeared on the scene
after hearing of his tragic losses: Eliphaz the Temanite, Bildad the Shuhite, and
Zophar the Naamathite. The purpose of their visit was to "mourn" with Job "and
to comfort him" (2:11). Incredibly, these three committed friends sat down with
Job "on the ground seven days and seven nights, and no one spoke a word to him,
for they saw that his grief was very great" (verse 13).

Job finally opens up his heart to his three companions. He laments the day
he was born, crying out, "Why did I not die at birth? Why did I not perish when
I came from the womb?" (3:11). Job continues to pour out his anguish and grief,
confiding that "the thing I greatly feared has come upon me, and what I dreaded
has happened to me" (verse 25).

Sadly, Job's friends offer little comfort in response. It was a common view even in the ancient world that blessings were caused by obedience and tragedy was caused by sin. Therefore, Job's friends advise him to remove himself from God's "doghouse" by confessing whatever sins had caused his losses. When Job protests that he has *not* violated his integrity, his friends push even harder for him to repent. What follows is an escalating debate in which Eliphaz and Bildad pressure Job to admit his wrongdoing while Job maintains his innocence.

KEYS TO THE TEXT

Read Job 4:1–6:30, noting the key words and phrases indicated below.

> *ELIPHAZ'S FIRST SPEECH: Job's friend offers his opinion on what caused Job's misery and what he should do to fix the situation.*

4:1. ELIPHAZ THE TEMANITE: Eliphaz speaks profoundly and gently, but again he knows nothing of the scene in heaven that had produced the suffering of Job.

7. WHO EVER PERISHED BEING INNOCENT: Eliphaz is likely trying to encourage Job by saying he won't die because he is innocent of any deadly iniquity. However, he concludes that Job must be guilty of *some* serious sin, because he was reaping anger from God.

12. A WORD WAS SECRETLY BROUGHT TO ME: Eliphaz bolsters his argument and viewpoint by claiming that a divine messenger had come to him in a vision, eerie fantasy, or a dream.

18. IF HE CHARGES HIS ANGELS WITH ERROR: The conclusion of Eliphaz's revelation is that Job suffered because he was not righteous enough. His message, in effect, is that God judges sin and sinners among people just as He does among the angels.

5:1. HOLY ONES: Angelic beings are in view. Eliphaz says that not even the angels could help Job. He must recognize his mortality and sin if he desires to be healed.

7. SPARKS: Literally this reads "the sons of Resheph," an expression that describes all sorts of fire-like movement (see, for example, Deuteronomy 32:24 and Psalm 78:48).

9. MARVELOUS THINGS WITHOUT NUMBER: The whole of Eliphaz's argument is based on the moral perfection of God, so he seeks to extoll God's greatness and goodness. However, his words lack the needed perspective of Scripture's special revelation.

17. HAPPY IS THE MAN WHOM GOD CORRECTS: Eliphaz puts a positive spin on his advice by telling Job that enviable or desirable is the situation of the person whom God cares enough about to chasten. His advice is that if Job would only admit his sin, he could be happy again.

19. HE SHALL DELIVER YOU: The language of this section, promising blessing for penitence, is reminiscent of Leviticus 26, which elaborates on the blessing of a faithful covenant relationship with God. If Job confessed, he would have prosperity, security, a family, and a rich life.

23. YOU SHALL HAVE A COVENANT: Eliphaz states that even the created order will be in harmony with the person whose relationship with God is corrected through His discipline.

> A JUST COMPLAINT: *Job answers Eliphaz by declaring that his punishment is not a result of his sin. Therefore, he is justified in seeking answers from God.*

6:2. OH, THAT MY GRIEF WERE FULLY WEIGHED: The heaviness of Job's burden—physical, mental, emotional, and spiritual—causes the rashness of his words in this passage.

4. THE ARROWS OF THE ALMIGHTY . . . TERRORS OF GOD: These figures of speech indicate that Job believed his trials were coming from God as a result of His judgment.

8. MY REQUEST: Job's request is that God would finish the process. For Job, death is desirable at this point, in that it will bring relief from the inevitable course of events.

9. CUT ME OFF: This metaphor is drawn from the imagery of a weaver, who cuts off the excess thread on the loom (see Isaiah 38:12).

10. NOT CONCEALED THE WORDS OF THE HOLY ONE: Job states that he had not been avoiding the revelation of God that he had received. God's commands are precious to him, and he has lived by them. He simply cannot find any source of sin as the cause of his intense suffering.

14. KINDNESS SHOULD BE SHOWN BY HIS FRIEND: Job rebukes his friends with these sage words. Even if a person had forsaken God (which he had not), should not his friends still show kindness to him? How can Eliphaz be so unkind as to continually indict him?

15. DECEITFULLY LIKE A BROOK: Job describes his friends as being about as useful with their counsel as a dry riverbed in summer.

19. TEMA . . . SHEBA: Tema, in the north, was named for the son of Ishmael (see Genesis 25:15). Sheba, in the south, was part of the Arabian desert, where water was precious.

24. CAUSE ME TO UNDERSTAND WHEREIN I HAVE ERRED: Job is not claiming here to be sinless. Rather, he is challenging his accusers: "If I've sinned, show me where!" Job is convinced there is no sin in his life that has led directly to the suffering he is enduring.

Read Job 8:1–9:35, noting the key words and phrases indicated below.

> A CALL TO REPENT: *Bildad, a second friend of Job, is also certain that Job has sinned. He chides Job for his stubbornness and urges him to repent to God for his sin.*

8:3. DOES THE ALMIGHTY PERVERT JUSTICE: Bildad takes Job's claims for innocence and applies them to his simplistic notion of retribution. He concludes that Job is accusing God of injustice as the Lord metes out His justice.

7. YOUR LATTER END WOULD INCREASE ABUNDANTLY: In fact, this would be Job's outcome (see 42:10–17). However, this would come about not because Job repented of some specific sin, but because he humbled himself before the sovereign and inscrutable will of God.

8. INQUIRE, PLEASE, OF THE FORMER AGE: Bildad appeals to past authorities (that is, godly ancestors who taught the same principle) that where there is suffering, there must be sin.

13. SO ARE THE PATHS OF ALL WHO FORGET GOD: Bildad supports his logic of cause-and-effect by drawing on illustrations from nature. He states again that not only has Job sinned, but he has surely forgotten God as well.

20. GOD WILL NOT CAST AWAY THE BLAMELESS: This comment from Bildad contains a veiled offer of hope. Job will be to able laugh again, but he must

first take steps to become blameless. Again, Bildad is unaware of the dialogue between God and Satan, and unaware that God has already pronounced Job "blameless" twice to heavenly beings (see 1:8; 2:3).

> LONGING FOR A MEDIATOR: *Job responds by mourning that there was no one who could act as a liaison between himself and God so that he could plead his case.*

9:1. HOW CAN A MAN BE RIGHTEOUS BEFORE GOD? Job, in a mood of deep despair, responds to Bildad's accusations with arguments surrounding God's nature. He also begins to rationalize about things which, he will later admit, he knows dangerously little. Job concludes that God is holy, wise, and strong—but he wonders if the Lord God is truly fair.

3. CONTEND WITH HIM: Job refers to disputing one's innocence or guilt before God as a useless endeavor. The psalmist would later illustrate the point: "If You, LORD, should mark iniquities [keep records of sin] . . . who could stand [innocent in judgment]?" (Psalm 130:3).

6. PILLARS TREMBLE: In the figurative language of the day, this phrase described the supporting power that secured the position of the earth in the universe.

9. BEAR, ORION, AND THE PLEIADES: Three stellar constellations.

THE CHAMBERS OF THE SOUTH: These were other constellations in the southern hemisphere, unseen by those who could view and name the three in the northern skies.

13. THE PROUD: Literally "Rahab," symbolic of an ancient mythological sea monster. God smiting the proud was a poetic way of saying that if the mythical monster of the sea (a metaphor for powerful, evil, chaotic forces) could not stand before God's anger, how could Job hope to do so? In a battle in God's court, he would lose.

15. THOUGH I WERE RIGHTEOUS: Job again does not mean that he is sinless, but that he has spiritual integrity (a pure heart to love, serve, and obey God). He is reaffirming for his friends that his suffering is not due to any sin that he is unwilling to confess.

24. COVERS THE FACES OF ITS JUDGES: Job here indicts God for the inequities of His world. He accuses God of treating everyone the same way, unfairly,

and of even covering the eyes of earthly judges so they will not see injustice. These are charges that later bring about God's rebuke of Job (see Job 38–41), and for which he eventually repents (see 42:1–6).

29. WHY THEN DO I LABOR IN VAIN? Job basically concludes, "God seems to have found me guilty, so why struggle? Even if I make every effort to clean every aspect of my life, the Lord will still punish me." This reflects his deep sense of despair and hopelessness in the moment.

32. THAT WE SHOULD GO TO COURT TOGETHER: Job acknowledges that as a mere man, he has no right to call on God to declare his innocence or to contend with God over his innocence. Job again did not believe that he had sinned to the extent that he deserved the severe suffering that he was facing. Job holds to the same simplistic system of retribution as that of his accusers—which held that all suffering was always caused by sin.

33. ANY MEDIATOR BETWEEN US: Job complains that there is no mediator—a court official who saw both sides clearly—to bring about resolution in his case. Where was an advocate, an arbitrator, an umpire, or a referee? Was there no one to remove God's rod and call for justice?

UNLEASHING THE TEXT

1) How would you summarize the primary theme of Eliphaz's words? What about Bildad's words?

_____

_____

_____

_____

_____

_____

2) Is it true that God punishes the guilty and blesses the righteous? Explain.

_____

_____

_____

_____

_____

3) Why is it significant that Job so earnestly desired a mediator to stand between himself and God to help him plead his case?

_____

_____

_____

_____

_____

_____

4) What was the core message of Job's responses to Eliphaz and Bildad? What was Job's primary complaint when he spoke directly to God?

_____

_____

_____

_____

_____

_____

EXPLORING THE MEANING

It is possible to be correct and harmful at the same time. Much of what Eliphaz and Bildad say is accurate—especially as it relates to God. Eliphaz rightly proclaims that God punishes the wicked for their sin (see 4:8–9). He adds that God is a fountain of goodness and mercy who is in sovereign control of the world (see 5:10–11). He extolls the wonders of God's forgiving nature: "Behold, happy is the man whom God corrects . . . He bruises, but He binds up; He wounds, but His hands make whole" (verses 17–18).

Similarly, Bildad's advice to Job would have been helpful if he had been correct about sin being the cause of Job's suffering. "Does God subvert judgment?" he asks, "Or does the Almighty pervert justice?" (8:3). Bildad urges Job to repent and seek God's forgiveness, proclaiming that "God will not cast away the blameless, nor will He uphold the evildoers" (verse 20). Again, all these basic sentiments from Bildad about God are accurate.

The problem is that both Eliphaz and Bildad are unaware of God's conversation with Satan in the throne room of heaven. They did not know of Satan's role in stripping Job of his family, his servants, his wealth, and his health. Job's friends spoke truth on an intellectual level, but their words caused harm because they failed to hear what Job was trying to say. They lacked empathy and true compassion. In this way, they serve as a negative example for Paul's admonition that we help one another by "speaking the truth in love" (Ephesians 4:15). Both are necessary when we approach anyone going through a season of suffering.

Life is rarely simplistic. People in the ancient world commonly believed that tragedies and suffering were the direct result of wicked or evil decisions. Those who suffered in a notable way were thought to have affronted the gods. Even within the community of those who worshiped the one true God, it was commonly believed that blessing was God's direct response to righteousness and trials were God's direct response to sin.

The Gospel of John offers an insightful illustration of this belief: "Now as Jesus passed by, He saw a man who was blind from birth. And His disciples asked Him, saying, 'Rabbi, who sinned, this man or his parents, that he was born blind?'" (9:1–2). The disciples believed that the man's blindness was caused by God's punishment—it was their natural assumption. They wanted Jesus to tell them whether it was the man or his parents who had rebelled against God in such a major way that had caused God to retaliate with blindness.

Jesus' answer was informative: "Neither this man nor his parents sinned, but that the works of God should be revealed in him" (verse 3). In other words, the traditional thinking of the day was not correct. Sin is not always the immediate cause of suffering. In reality, things rarely operate according to the black-and-white boundaries put forward by Eliphaz and Bildad. Both our physical lives and our spiritual lives are much more complicated—a truth we need to keep in mind when we encounter those who have experienced tragedy.

Humanity needs a mediator. Job responded to Bildad's call to repent by lamenting the distance he felt between himself and God. He extolled God's majesty, power, and righteousness, and then he asked, "How then can I answer Him, and choose my words to reason with Him?" (9:14). Job longed to make his case before God as his Judge. Yet he felt as if he had no access to the Almighty—no way to approach Him and beg for mercy.

Job's description of his plight near the end of chapter 9 is especially poignant: "For He is not a man, as I am, that I may answer Him, and that we should go to court together. Nor is there any mediator between us, who may lay his hand on us both" (verses 32–33). Without realizing it, Job was pointing forward to the work of Jesus as the Messiah.

Paul would later emphasize this element of Jesus' ministry when he wrote, "For there is one God and one Mediator between God and men, the Man Christ Jesus, who gave Himself a ransom for all, to be testified in due time" (1 Timothy 2:5–6). On the cross, Jesus accepted the wages of sin—death. Thus, He paid the price of redemption for all who believe. Therefore, Scripture says, "He is also able to save to the uttermost those who come to God through Him, since He always lives to make intercession for them" (Hebrews 7:25), and, "if anyone sins, we have an Advocate with the Father, Jesus Christ the righteous" (1 John 2:1). In other words, Christ has provided exactly what Job longed to find.

REFLECTING ON THE TEXT

5) How have people tried to offer comfort or compassion to you during a season of suffering? In what ways were their actions helpful or harmful?

_____

_____

_____

_____

_____

6) Why is it so easy to believe that bad things happen because of bad choices and good things happen because of good choices?

_____

_____

_____

_____

7) When have you felt distant or disconnected from God?

_____

_____

_____

_____

_____

8) Jesus is the Mediator between God and humanity. How has that truth influenced your life?

_____

_____

_____

_____

_____

PERSONAL RESPONSE

9) What are some practical and helpful ways that you can offer both truth and love when people close to you are hurting?

_____

_____

_____

_____

_____

10) Jesus exists as a Mediator between you and a holy God. How will you take advantage of that truth this week?

_____

_____

_____

_____

_____

3

ANSWERING THE CRITICS
Job 11:1–14:22

DRAWING NEAR
What are some subjects about which you enjoy an argument or debate?

_____

_____

_____

_____

_____

_____

THE CONTEXT
In the previous lesson, we witnessed the first interactions between Job and the friends who came to comfort him in his time of trouble. Unfortunately for Job, there was not a lot of comfort being offered. Instead, Eliphaz and Bildad pressured Job to acknowledge that his suffering had been caused by sin or rebellion against God that Job had kept secret.

Job 4–10 established a pattern in which one of Job's companions makes a speech or implores Job to repent, and then Job responds to their arguments and offers his own rebuttal. Then another friend speaks, and Job again responds to their words. We see this same pattern on display in Job 11–14, except this time the conversation is between Job and his third companion, Zophar the Naamathite.

The back-and-forth between Zophar and Job has a sharp and personal feel to it. Both men resort to sarcasm and bitter words in their effort to get their points across. Finally, after addressing Zophar, Job again casts his eyes toward

God and speaks directly to Him—searching for answers and reasons for his suffering.

KEYS TO THE TEXT

Read Job 11:1–14:22, noting the key words and phrases indicated below.

> ANOTHER INTERROGATION: *Job's third friend, Zophar, steps off the sideline to throw both questions and accusations at Job's feet.*

11.1. ZOPHAR THE NAAMATHITE: This friend now steps in to interrogate Job and assault him using the same basic law of retaliation. Job must repent, he says, again not understanding the heavenly reality that is at work. He is indignant at Job's protests of innocence.

2. SHOULD A MAN FULL OF TALK BE VINDICATED: The allegations against Job now move to a new level. According to Zophar, not only is Job guilty and unrepentant, but he is also an empty talker. In fact, in Zophar's mind, his friend's long-winded defense of his innocence and God's apparent injustice is a sin that is worthy of rebuke.

4. CLEAN IN YOUR EYES: As we have seen, Job never claims sinlessness. But he does maintain that he is innocent of any great transgression or attitude of unrepentance, reaffirming his sincerity and integrity as a man of faith and obedience to God. This claim infuriates Zophar, and he wishes that God Himself would confirm the accusations of Job's friends.

6. SECRETS OF WISDOM: The claim is that Job would have been wiser if he had only known the unknowable secrets of God. In this case, the scene in heaven would have clarified everything. But Job couldn't know that secret wisdom of God. Zophar should have applied his point to himself. If God's wisdom is so deep, high, long, and broad, how is it that he could understand it and have all the answers? Like his friends, Zophar thought he understood God. He reverted to the same law of retaliation, the sowing and reaping principle, to again indict Job.

13. PREPARE YOUR HEART: Zophar sets out four steps to Job's repentance: (1) devote your heart to God, (2) stretch your hands to Him in prayer for forgiveness, (3) put your sin far away, and (4) don't allow any sin in your tent. If Job did these things, he would be blessed. If Job did not repent, he would die. Zophar was right that faith in God is based on confession of sins and obedience. But, like his

friends, he was wrong in not understanding that God allows unpredictable and seemingly unfair suffering for reasons not known on earth.

20. THE EYES OF THE WICKED WILL FAIL: Zophar started out this section speaking directly to Job ("If you would . . .") and concluded speaking proverbially ("the eyes of the wicked . . ."). In so doing, Zophar avoids directly calling Job wicked, but succeeds with even greater force by being indirect. In the end, he tells Job that his sin will bring about his own death.

> THE END OF ROUND ONE: *Job again refuted the idea that all suffering is a retaliation for individual sin, ending the first cycle between himself and his friends.*

12:2. WISDOM WILL DIE WITH YOU: Job responds with cutting sarcasm directed at his know-it-all friends. He states that he understands the principles about which they have spoken, but he concludes that those principles are irrelevant to his situation. On top of that, he despairs at the pain of becoming a derision to his friends—though he is innocent of their charges.

4. I AM . . . JUST AND BLAMELESS: This may sound like presumption on Job's part, but it is actually the same pronouncement that God made about him (see 1:8; 2:3).

5. A LAMP IS DESPISED: As a torch is to a wanderer, so Job was to his friends. When all was at ease with them, they didn't need him. They even mocked him.

6. GOD PROVIDES: Job refutes the simplistic idea that the righteous always prosper and the wicked always suffer by reminding his friends that God allows thieves and sinners to be prosperous and secure. So why not believe that God may also allow the righteous to suffer?

7–8. THE BEASTS . . . THE BIRDS . . . THE EARTH . . . THE FISH: Job uses all these elements of creation (animals, birds, plants, and fish) as illustrations that the violent often prosper and live securely. God has made it so the more vicious survive.

12. WISDOM IS WITH AGED MEN: The interrogative nature of the preceding verse may carry over to make this a question from Job: "Shouldn't aged men be wise?" If this is the reading, it represents a stinging sarcasm against his aged friends who gave him such unwise advice. They spoke and heard only what suited them.

13. WITH HIM ARE WISDOM AND STRENGTH: Job, in spite of his questions about his suffering, affirms that God's power is visible in nature, human society, religious matters, and international affairs. However, he expresses this in terms of fatalistic despair.

13:3. I WOULD SPEAK TO THE ALMIGHTY: Job does not want to argue with his friends anymore. Instead, he wants to take his case directly before God.

4. YOU FORGERS OF LIES: Yet Job cannot hold back from another blistering denunciation of his useless counselors, telling them their silence would be true wisdom.

7. WICKEDLY FOR GOD ... DECEITFULLY FOR HIM: Job accuses his friends of using lies and fallacies to vindicate God when they assert that he was a sinner because he was a sufferer.

8. WILL YOU CONTEND FOR GOD: Job is basically asking his friends if they are wise enough to argue in God's defense. To take such an attitude is brash, mocks God by misrepresenting Him, and should lead to fear of chastening from the Almighty.

14. TAKE MY FLESH IN MY TEETH: A proverb meaning, "Why should I anxiously desire to save my life?" Job is saying that he could try to preserve his life, just like an animal who holds its prey in its mouth to preserve it, but this is not his motive.

15. THOUGH HE SLAY ME, YET WILL I TRUST HIM: Job assures his accusers that his convictions are not self-serving, because he is ready to die trusting in God. But still, he will defend his innocence before the Lord, and he is confident that he is truly saved and not a hypocrite.

17–19. DECLARATION ... CASE ... VINDICATED ... CONTEND: The language of a courtroom comes out strongly in Job's defense. He cannot just be silent and die.

> *JOB'S PRAYER: Job asks God to end his pain and remove the terrors that he is facing. He is concerned with his misery but also his relationship with God.*

21. WITHDRAW YOUR HAND: Job wants God to end his pain and speak to him.

23. HOW MANY ARE MY INIQUITIES AND SINS? Job desires to know the answer to this question so he can determine if his measure of suffering matches the severity of his sin. He could then repent of any sins about which he was unaware.

26. WRITE BITTER THINGS AGAINST ME: This is a judicial phrase referring to the writing down of a sentence against a criminal. Job uses it figuratively here to describe his extreme suffering, as if it were a divine sentence as just punishment for extreme sin. Job feels that God might be punishing him for sins committed years earlier in his youth.

27. WATCH CLOSELY ALL MY PATHS. In another context, these words speak of protection. But here Job questions whether God has not held him on too tight a leash. The comment amounts to saying that God is being overly rigorous toward Job's sin as compared to others.

LIFE's WOES: Job concludes his response to Zophar by reflecting on the plight of humans and asks God to extend grace to him.

28. MAN DECAYS LIKE A ROTTEN THING: This general comment on the plight of humans should not be separated from Job 14:1, which it introduces.

14:1–12. MAN . . . IS OF FEW DAYS: Job embraces the fact that God is in control over the issues of life, but he challenges their meaning. Life is short (see verses 1–2), all people are sinners (see verse 4), the days of humans are limited (see verse 5), and then comes death (verses 7–12). In light of this, Job asks God for grace instead of intense judgment (see verse 3), and a little rest from all the pain (see verse 6). He suggests that a tree has more hope than he does at the present moment (see verse 7).

13. HIDE ME IN THE GRAVE: Job asks to die and remain in the grave until God's anger is over, and then be raised to life again when God calls him back.

16. YOU NUMBER MY STEPS: Job reasons that if he were dead, God wouldn't be watching his every step and counting his every sin—it would all be hidden. Here is the hope of resurrection for those who trust God. Job has hope that if he dies, he will live again.

19. YOU DESTROY THE HOPE OF MAN: Job now returns to his complaint before God and reverts to his former hopeless mood, speaking about death as inevitable and causing separation. He is painfully sad to think of it.

UNLEASHING THE TEXT

1) What does it mean for a person to *repent*?

_____

_____

_____

_____

2) How would you describe the basic thrust of Zophar's argument?

_____

_____

_____

3) Look again at Job 12:4–12. What lesson did Job want his companions to learn from thieves, beasts, and birds?

_____

_____

_____

_____

4) Was it right or wrong for Job to hope for death in the middle of his plight? Explain.

_____

_____

_____

EXPLORING THE MEANING

Repentance is the correct response to sin. One of the primary themes mentioned by all three of Job's companions is the need for repentance. It is worth mentioning that as a general principle, repentance *is* the best response whenever we find ourselves living in rebellion against God or making choices that contradict with His will. "If we confess our sins, He is faithful and just to forgive us our sins and to cleanse us from all unrighteousness" (1 John 1:9).

Zophar provides a four-step process for repentance to Job. First, he says to "prepare your heart" (11:13). This means to consciously stop what we are doing, examine our hearts, and let go of what should not be there. Second, "stretch out your hands toward [God]" (verse 13). Sin always separates us from God. Therefore, a necessary part of repentance is intentionally reaching out to God by turning away from sin and back toward Him. Third, identify any iniquity and "put it far away" (verse 14). When we repent of sin, we must discontinue that sin. We must do whatever is necessary to stop those behaviors and put them "far away."

Finally, Zophar advises Job to "not let wickedness dwell in your tents" (verse 14). In other words, we must be vigilant to prevent the return of any sinful patterns. We must set a guard in our hearts and minds to keep out what has caused us trouble in the past. Accountability with others is a useful tool in this process. So, as we see, Zophar was wrong in his stubborn belief that Job was living in conscious rebellion against God. But his instructions on how to repent are helpful if we do ever find ourselves in that kind of rebellion.

God is a worthy Judge. If there is one thing about which Job and his companions could agree, it was the greatness and majesty of God. All four men affirmed multiple times in their discourses that God is worthy of praise, that He judges rightly, and that His thoughts and judgments are beyond criticism because they are beyond our human ability to comprehend.

"Can you search out the deep things of God?" Zophar asked. "Can you find out the limits of the Almighty? They are higher than heaven—what can you do? Deeper than Sheol—what can you know? Their measure is longer than the earth and broader than the sea" (11:7–8). Zophar understood that God cannot be contained or corralled.

"With [God] are wisdom and strength," Job answered. "He has counsel and understanding" (12:13). "With Him are strength and prudence," he added (verse 16). And, "He uncovers deep things out of darkness, and brings the shadow of death to light. He makes nations great, and destroys them; He enlarges nations, and guides them" (verses 22–23).

Both men understood that God is worthy to judge humanity because He is wise and powerful beyond measure.

It is appropriate to express our emotions to God. For most of the conversations between Job and his friends, Job addresses his responses and rebuttals to his companions. He speaks first to Eliphaz, and then to Bildad, and then to Zophar. At times, however, Job turns his attention and his words directly to God. These words are included in the second half of Job 14.

What does Job say to God in those verses? Primarily, he expresses the deep and bitter anguish of his soul. "Oh, that You would hide me in the grave," he says, speaking to God. "That You would conceal me until Your wrath is past, that You would appoint me a set time, and remember me!" (verse 13). He expresses to God his confusion and frustration with everything that has happened to him. Job feels as if God has destroyed his hope in the same way that rockslides destroy a mountain slope and water wears away stone (verses 18–19).

Job was not being melodramatic in these expressions, nor was he making accusations or casting aspersions toward God. Instead, he was openly and honestly pouring himself out to the Lord, believing and trusting that God had heard him. When we feel hopeless, frustrated, or angry about our circumstances, we don't help ourselves by pushing those feelings down and trying to act pious or "spiritual." We do better to cry out to God, just as Job did. After all, the Lord already knows what we are feeling! And He has the power to bring comfort and peace.

REFLECTING ON THE TEXT

5) When have you gone through the process of repenting of a choice or series of choices? What happened in your life as a result of going through that process?

_____

_____

_____

_____

_____

6) What are obstacles that tend to hinder your ability to repent when you sin?

_____

_____

_____

_____

7) What are some ways that you have seen God's wisdom and power intersect directly with your life?

_____

_____

_____

_____

_____

_____

8) Do you find it easy or difficult to express your emotions to God? What about when you feel angry or frustrated with God? Explain.

_____

_____

_____

_____

_____

PERSONAL RESPONSE

9) Are there any areas of sin or rebellion against God about which you need to repent? If so, what are those areas?

_____

_____

_____

_____

_____

_____

10) What steps can you take to better express your thoughts and feelings to God this week?

_____

_____

_____

_____

_____

_____

4

An Accusation of Folly
Job 15:1–17:16

Drawing Near
How do you tend to react when you sense someone is being sarcastic toward you?

_____

_____

_____

_____

_____

_____

_____

_____

The Context
In the previous two lessons, we examined what scholars often call the "first cycle" of conversations between Job and his three companions. These conversations follow a specific pattern. First, one of Job's three friends speaks out, trying to convince Job that his personal sin and rebellion against God must be the cause of his suffering. Next, Job responds to these accusations and offers a rebuttal. Then another friend speaks, and Job answers that complaint.

Job 15 begins the "second cycle" of these conversations. This next round mirrors the first in many ways, with Eliphaz, Bildad, and Zophar still pushing for Job to repent, and Job standing firm on his innocence before God. However, the intensity increases as the men become more and more entrenched in their arguments. They begin to accuse Job of folly for not heeding their advice. As Eliphaz states, "Should a wise man answer with empty knowledge, and fill himself with the east wind?" (15:2).

Job 17 represents a notable exception to this pattern. In this chapter, Job again turns his gaze upward and speaks directly to God. His words are poignant and his desire for relief of his suffering evident—including the suffering of enduring such painful "comfort" from his friends.

KEYS TO THE TEXT
Read Job 15:1–17:16, noting the key words and phrases indicated below.

> *ACCUSATIONS OF FOLLY: Eliphaz declares that Job is acting foolishly by rejecting the conventional wisdom of their day.*

15:1: THEN ELIPHAZ THE TEMANITE ANSWERED: Eliphaz views Job's suffering as the result of God's divine punishment against him for sin, stating, "Those who plow iniquity and sow trouble reap the same" (Job 4:8). He now initiates the second cycle of speeches between Job and his three friends. As we will discover, Job's resistance to their viewpoint and his appeals have energized them to even greater intensity in their confrontation.

5. YOUR INIQUITY TEACHES YOUR MOUTH: Eliphaz begins by accusing Job of sinning due to the complaints that Job has just voiced to God. He feels Job is guilty of empty words and has not exhibited godly fear and righteousness in his prayer, but rather was sinning with his words.

7. ARE YOU THE FIRST MAN WHO WAS BORN? Eliphaz next condemns Job for rejecting conventional wisdom, as if he has more insight than other people. He asks, "What do you know that we do not know? What do you understand that is not in us?" (verse 9).

11. ARE THE CONSOLATIONS OF GOD TOO SMALL FOR YOU: Eliphaz next accuses Job of rejecting the wisdom of the aged (see verse 10; see also 12:12) and the kindness of God.

14. WHAT IS MAN, THAT HE COULD BE PURE? A strong statement from Eliphaz in regard to the general sinfulness of man. As Paul would later write, "All have sinned and fall short of the glory of God" (Romans 3:23). Eliphaz makes the comment here to attack Job's claim to righteousness.

15. THE HEAVENS ARE NOT PURE IN HIS SIGHT: This refers to the holy angels who were persuaded by Lucifer (the devil) to rebel and brought impurity into the heavens. As Isaiah wrote, "How you are fallen from heaven, O Lucifer, son of the morning! How you are cut down to the ground, you who weakened the nations!" (14:12, see also Revelation 12:3–4).

16. MAN . . . IS ABOMINABLE AND FILTHY: The truth of Eliphaz's statement is accurate—all men are sinners—but irrelevant in Job's case, for his suffering was not due to any sin.

17. WHAT I HAVE SEEN I WILL DECLARE: Eliphaz once again returns to the perspective that he held before: Job's suffering has come about as a result of sin that he has committed.

20. THE WICKED MAN WRITHES WITH PAIN: Eliphaz supports his relentless point by launching into a lengthy monologue about the wicked and their outcomes in life, which includes many parallels to Job's sufferings. Eliphaz begins by noting that a wicked man "writhes with pain" and does not know when his life will end.

21. DREADFUL SOUNDS . . . THE DESTROYER COMES: The wicked man suffers from fear. Every sound alarms him, and he thinks his destroyer is near.

23. HE WANDERS ABOUT FOR BREAD: The wicked man worries about having food.

25. HE STRETCHES OUT HIS HAND AGAINST GOD: The wicked man's suffering causes him to question God.

30. THE FLAME WILL DRY OUT HIS BRANCHES: The wicked man, though once well nourished, housed, and rich, will end up losing it all. He will dry up like a branch under a flame.

34. THE COMPANY OF HYPOCRITES: Eliphaz concludes his second speech by calling Job a hypocrite. He tells his friend that this is the reason things are going so badly for him.

A PRAYER FOR RELIEF: Job continues to reject the reproaches of his companions. He then turns to God and asks for relief from his suffering.

16:2. MISERABLE COMFORTERS ARE YOU ALL: Job's friends had come to comfort him, and at first they had supported him by being with him for seven blissful days of silence. But their mission has failed miserably, for their comfort has only turned into more torment for Job.

3. WHAT PROVOKES YOU THAT YOU ANSWER? What had started out as Eliphaz's sincere efforts to help Job understand his dilemma had turned into rancor and sarcasm. In the end, their haranguing had heightened the frustrations of all parties involved.

4. IF YOUR SOUL WERE IN MY SOUL'S PLACE: Job states that if the matter were reversed and he were in the role of comforter to his friends, he would never treat them as they had treated him. Rather, he would seek to strengthen and comfort them.

9. HE TEARS ME IN HIS WRATH: Job laments that his sufferings are severe judgments from God, who has worn him out and chewed him up by severe scrutiny.

MY ADVERSARY SHARPENS HIS GAZE ON ME: Job continues by referring to God as "my adversary," who has shattered, shaken, shot at, and sliced him (see verses 12–14)..

19. SURELY EVEN NOW MY WITNESS IS IN HEAVEN: Job has no one to turn to in his sorrow except God, who is silent in heaven and has not vindicated him.

21. PLEAD FOR A MAN WITH GOD: This pleading would be for a verdict of innocent on behalf of a friend or neighbor in a court setting before the judge. God anticipated the need of an advocate, and He provided One in the person of the Lord Jesus Christ. The apostle Paul wrote, "For there is one God and one Mediator between God and men, the Man Christ Jesus" (1 Timothy 2:5). John added, "My little children, these things I write to you, so that you may not sin. And if anyone sins, we have an Advocate with the Father, Jesus Christ the righteous" (1 John 2:1).

A PRAYER FOR DELIVERANCE: Job concludes his prayer for relief by condemning his friends for their remarks and stating that his deliverance will be found in God alone.

17:2. MOCKERS WITH ME: Job's would-be counselors have become his actual enemies and the provocation for his tears.

3. PUT DOWN A PLEDGE: Job calls on God to promise (by a symbolic handshake) that his case will be heard in the heavenly court.

4. NOT EXALT THEM: Job recognizes that his friends' blindness toward his innocence comes from God, so he asks that the Lord would not let them succeed in their efforts against him.

5. HE WHO SPEAKS FLATTERY: This Hebrew term came to mean "prey." Job is thus referring to someone who delivers up a friend as prey to some enemy.

6. A BYWORD OF THE PEOPLE: This refers to shame, reproach, and a reputation that is extremely bad. As Moses told the people of Israel, if they disobeyed God, they would become "an astonishment, a proverb, and a byword among all nations" (Deuteronomy 28:37).

IN WHOSE FACE MEN SPIT: This is the most disdainful act a person could commit in Job's day, to heap scorn and shame on someone as a wicked and unworthy person. Job is saying that his friends are aiding him in getting such a reputation.

9. YET THE RIGHTEOUS WILL HOLD TO HIS WAY: Job, and other righteous people who find themselves in a similar situation, must remain righteous. If they do, Job knows the suffering will produce strength. As Paul later wrote, "[God] said to me, 'My grace is sufficient for you, for My strength is made perfect in weakness.' Therefore most gladly I will rather boast in my infirmities, that the power of Christ may rest upon me" (2 Corinthians 12:9).

10. COME BACK AGAIN, ALL OF YOU: Job was not unteachable. He invites his friends to speak again if they have something wise to say, for a change, but not to talk about his restoration.

15. WHERE THEN IS MY HOPE? Job's hope was in God alone.

16. GATES OF SHEOL: A reference to death. Jesus also referred to these gates when He said to Peter, "You are Peter, and on this rock I will build My church, and the gates of Hades shall not prevail against it" (Matthew 16:18).

UNLEASHING THE TEXT

1) Eliphaz accused Job of sinning in the complaints he voiced to God. Do you agree or disagree with Elipahz's line of thinking? Explain.

_____

_____

_____

_____

_____

2) Eliphaz argued passionately that the wicked are forced to endure terrible punishments in this life. How does that argument compare and contrast with reality today?

_____
_____
_____
_____
_____
_____

3) What reasons did Job have to feel frustrated by his companions?

_____
_____
_____
_____
_____
_____

4) What were some of the reasons Job expressed for his frustration with God?

_____
_____
_____
_____
_____
_____

EXPLORING THE MEANING

The wicked do not always suffer in this life. The conventional wisdom of the ancient world said that extreme suffering was always a punishment for extreme rebellion against the gods—or in Job's case, rebellion against *the* God. This was the message that Eliphaz, Bildad, and Zophar had taken pains to communicate during the first cycle of their conversation with Job.

Eliphaz hammers that same nail to begin the second cycle. "The wicked man writhes with pain all his days," he says, "and the number of years is hidden from the oppressor" (15:20). He adds, "Trouble and anguish make him afraid; they overpower him, like a king ready for battle. For he stretches out his hand against God, and acts defiantly against the Almighty" (verses 24–25). In fact, the entire second half of Job 15 is filled with these kinds of arguments.

The problem, of course, is that these statements don't stand up against real life. When we look at the world today, we see plenty of wicked and evil people who not only seem to avoid suffering but who also appear to live in the lap of luxury. There have been many famous examples throughout history of men and women who rejected God and oppressed the helpless over their entire lives—yet seemed to experience no adverse consequences.

This was true in biblical times as well. "Why does the way of the wicked prosper?" Jeremiah pondered. "Why are those happy who deal so treacherously?" (Jeremiah 12:1). The unrighteous in this life do not always feel the consequences of their wickedness in this life.

The righteous do not always receive blessings in this life. Conventional wisdom in the ancient world also held that righteous people—those who were faithful in their worship *and* faithful to care for the poor and needy—received blessings because of their righteousness. These blessings were believed to be material, relational, spiritual, and intellectual (wisdom).

Most of Job's life had conformed with the conventional wisdom of his day. As we have seen, he was known as "blameless and upright, and one who feared God and shunned evil" (1:1). He was righteous and had been blessed by God to the extreme: "His possessions were seven thousand sheep, three thousand camels, five hundred yoke of oxen, five hundred female donkeys, and a very large household, so that this man was the greatest of all the people of the East" (verse 3).

In short, Job was an ideal example of the belief that goodness always produces blessing—until everything came crashing down. Readers of Job's story understand Satan's role in causing Job's suffering, and that God allowed Satan to move against him. This truth proves that those who choose to obey God and lead righteous and godly lives will not always be compensated with blessings for their obedience.

Jesus Himself was perfectly righteous in every way, yet He experienced untold suffering on the cross. He also warned His followers that suffering would come their way—not in spite of their decision to follow Him, but *because* of it. "In the world you will have tribulation; but be of good cheer, I have overcome the world" (John 16:33).

God will ultimately judge the wicked and the righteous. Conventional wisdom says that what we reap in this life we will sow in this life. This is a biblical principle, for as Paul stated, "Do not be deceived, God is not mocked; for whatever a man sows, that he will also reap" (Galatians 6:7). Our actions always have consequences, whether positive or negative. But sometimes the situations we face do not come about as a direct result of something we have done. As we saw in Job's case, unseen spiritual forces are constantly at work against the people of God (see Ephesians 6:12).

The reality, as we have seen, is that sometimes the wicked prosper in this life, and sometimes the righteous suffer in this life. The key to those statements is *in this life*. In every situation, we can say with certainty that God will ultimately judge every person in a way that is just and right.

David recognized this. Psalm 17, for example, is a lament to God about the apparent dominance and relatively easy life of wicked men who were seeking his destruction—men "whose belly You fill with Your hidden treasure. They are satisfied with children, and leave the rest of their possession for their babes" (verse 14). But that verse starts by pointing out that they are "men of the world who have their portion *in this life*." That's all the blessing they will ever have. David looked forward to something better—an eternal reward: "As for me, I will see Your face in righteousness; I shall be satisfied when I awake in Your likeness" (verse 15).

God is the ultimate judge for humanity, and he promises to balance the scales of justice. The wonderful news of the gospel is that justice has been turned in favor of the sinner who repents and puts his trust in the Lord: "He is faithful and just to forgive us our sins and to cleanse us from all unrighteousness" (1 John 1:9). Because Christ has paid the price of atonement for our sin, we can receive the unfathomable blessing of eternal life. This comes not because of our own righteousness but solely because of the sacrifice that Jesus made for us on the cross.

REFLECTING ON THE TEXT

5) What does modern conventional wisdom say about the causes of blessings and tragedies?

6) When have you felt like you were being punished by God for your sins?

7) When have you fallen into the trap of striving to grow or deepen your relationship with God simply by behaving better? What was the result of pursuing that course of action?

8) Knowing that God is perfectly just, yet full of mercy and forgiveness toward those who repent and trust Him, how does that affect your view of sin?

PERSONAL RESPONSE

9) Are you currently in a season of blessing or a season of trial? Explain.

_____

_____

_____

_____

_____

_____

10) How can you use your current season as a way to share the gospel with those around you?

_____

_____

_____

_____

_____

_____

_____

5

A DISCOURSE ON THE WICKED
Job 18:1–21:34

DRAWING NEAR
How do you tend to handle people who keep pushing the same ideas or the same advice without really hearing what you have to say?

_____

_____

_____

_____

_____

_____

_____

_____

THE CONTEXT
We saw in the previous session that the second cycle of conversations between Job and his companions was more intense and personal than the first cycle. Eliphaz did not change much in terms of his arguments, continuing to drive home his belief that Job must be harboring some deep-seated sin for him to be suffering so much in his life. Yet Eliphaz did become more aggressive in his attacks against Job's character—and even his intelligence.

In a similar way, Bildad and Zophar now ramp up their rhetoric in their speeches during this second cycle. Bildad focuses primarily on his repeated claim that evil people always receive the consequences of their evil actions. Zophar expounds on the same theme, delivering essentially a sermon on the principle that God punishes the wicked.

For his part, Job continues to maintain his innocence before God. He also continues to appeal to God as both his witness and Judge. One striking moment can be found in Job 19, where Job declares his faith that a Redeemer lives who will vindicate him in the end. His language and his imagery are poignant pictures that foreshadow the work of Christ.

KEYS TO THE TEXT
Read Job 18:1–21:34, noting the key words and phrases indicated below.

> *BILDAD'S SECOND SPEECH: Like Eliphaz, Bildad ruthlessly attacks Job, telling him to stop complaining and start acting sensibly.*

3. WHY ARE WE COUNTED AS BEASTS? Bildad opens his second speech with scorn, asking Job why he is so firmly discounting their words. He will soon turn to another long tale of the bad outcomes that the wicked experience to support his points.

4. SHALL THE EARTH BE FORSAKEN FOR YOU? Bildad is speaking metaphorically here, to convey how radically Job is challenging prevailing wisdom. Bildad firmly believes it is only the wicked who suffer—so suffering can only come about as a result of wickedness.

5. THE LIGHT OF THE WICKED INDEED GOES OUT: Bildad's concern is to establish that every wicked person is paid in full. He is perhaps reacting to Job's comment that "the tents of robbers prosper, and those who provoke God are secure" (12:6). Bildad stresses to Job the doctrine of retribution—that the "light of the wicked" is indeed always snuffed out by God.

13. THE FIRSTBORN OF DEATH DEVOURS HIS LIMBS: A poetical expression meaning the most deadly disease that death ever produced. The description speaks not only of a progressive disease but also of the total destruction of the body in the grave.

14. THE KING OF TERRORS: Bildad personifies death, depicting all its terrors to the ungodly. He is perhaps drawing on imagery of the Canaanite god Mot, who was a devouring deity. Isaiah would later reverse the image, portraying God as swallowing up death (see Isaiah 25:8).

21. WHO DOES NOT KNOW GOD: This describes "know" in a redemptive sense and is here applied to an unbeliever. Bildad thus ends his remarks with a stunning insinuation. Not only does he consider Job guilty of wicked deeds, but he also implies that Job has no knowledge of God.

A DESPERATE CRY: Increasingly worn down by the stinging attacks of his companions, Job calls out for pity from both God and men.

19:1. HOW LONG WILL YOU TORMENT MY SOUL: Job responds to Bildad with an anguished cry that his friends have become recalcitrant and relentless toward him. They have had no effect on his dealing with the sin they imagine to be present in his life.

4. MY ERROR REMAINS WITH ME: Literally, "my error lives with me." Job implies that his friends have no right to interfere in his situation or behave as if they were God.

5–6. IF INDEED YOU EXALT YOURSELVES AGAINST ME . . . KNOW THEN THAT GOD HAS WRONGED ME: Job confesses that if God had sent him friends like Bildad, then what they are saying was true—God *has* wronged him. After all, with friends like them, who needs enemies?

8. HE HAS SET DARKNESS IN MY PATHS: Job turns in this next section to rehearsing his own suffering. God has closed him in, stripped him, broken him, and turned against him.

12. HIS TROOPS COME TOGETHER: Job pictures God's actions in military terms, much like a mighty army laying siege to a weakened city. Job feels that God's "troops" have advanced, built up a siege rampart, and encamped around his "tent." IIn truth, Job's perspective is not too far off—though it is *Satan*, not God, who has devised and unleashed these attacks on Job.

15. I AM AN ALIEN IN THEIR SIGHT: Job's family and friends have failed him. The rejection of one's family is devastating in any culture and any period of time. However, this was especially painful in the patriarchal society in which Job lived. There was little worse for a patriarch than to have his own children ridicule him as their father. Job has no one to support him.

20. I HAVE ESCAPED BY THE SKIN OF MY TEETH: This was the origin of the common slang phrase, "by the skin of my teeth," referring to skin that is thin and fragile. The idea is that Job has escaped death by a very slim margin. The loss

of all his family, as well as the abuse of his friends, has added to the terror of God-forsakenness which has gripped him.

23–24. MY WORDS WERE . . . ENGRAVED ON A ROCK: It is at this point of Job's greatest despair, when he feels totally abandoned and alone, that his faith appears at its highest level. Job wishes the activities of his life were put into words and inscribed in granite, as it were, so all would know that he has not sinned to the magnitude of his suffering. God ultimately granted this prayer.

25. I KNOW THAT MY REDEEMER LIVES: Job confidently affirms God's identity as his Redeemer (see Exodus 6:6). He wants that confidence in the record, so to speak, for all to know. God is his Redeemer and will vindicate him in that last day of judgment on the earth, when justice is perfectly and finally accomplished.

26. IN MY FLESH I SHALL SEE GOD: Job has no hope left for this life. However, he is confident that after he is dead, his Redeemer will vindicate him in the glory of a physical resurrection ("in my flesh"), in which he will enjoy perfect fellowship with the Redeemer. That Jesus Christ is the Redeemer of whom Job spoke is the clear message of the gospel (see Luke 2:38; Romans 3:24; Galatians 3:13; Ephesians 1:7; Hebrews 9:12).

> ZOPHAR'S SECOND SPEECH: Still entrenched in the conventional wisdom, Zophar hammers Job again with the claim that only the wicked suffer.

20:1. MY ANXIOUS THOUGHTS MAKE ME ANSWER: Zophar evidently takes Job's closing words as a personal affront. Zophar comes across as the most emotional of the three friends, and his "anxious thoughts" make him unwilling to allow Job's rebuke to go unanswered.

5. THE TRIUMPHING OF THE WICKED IS SHORT: Zophar cannot abide the thought that the wicked do prosper. It is likely his view is based on the fact that he is a prosperous and healthy man, which would lend support (and proof) to his claim that the righteous prosper. For Zophar, even if it seems as if the wicked are prospering, it is only brief and for a moment.

6. HIS HAUGHTINESS MOUNTS UP TO THE HEAVENS: The application of Zophar's words about this wicked, hypocritical, proud person are aimed at Job.

Job will—just like others who are wicked—ultimately suffer the consequences of his sins.

10. HIS CHILDREN WILL SEEK THE FAVOR OF THE POOR: Oppressing the poor was the mark of the truly wicked person. Job does not dispute this point, but he denies being such a person.

11. IT WILL LIE DOWN WITH HIM IN THE DUST: In other words, the wicked die young.

14. HIS FOOD IN HIS STOMACH TURNS SOUR: The evil man's wicked deeds (especially robbing the poor) may please his palate but will ultimately turn sour in his stomach. God "casts them out of his belly" and forces him to vomit up such ill-gained riches (verse 15).

17. HE WILL NOT SEE THE STREAMS: Evil in a life takes away all enjoyment. Zophar basically implies here again that Job has no joy in life because of his sin.

29. THIS IS THE PORTION FROM GOD FOR A WICKED MAN: Zophar concludes that more than just losing the enjoyment of life by sin, the wicked fall under the fury of God.

JOB APPEALS TO COMMON SENSE: Job takes a step back and reminds Zophar and the others that sometimes wicked people do prosper—which means they should understand that sometimes righteous people do suffer.

21:1. LISTEN CAREFULLY TO MY SPEECH: Job calls for his friends at this point to be quiet and pay attention to his words. It is likely that he makes this request because so far they have not really been listening to him. They just keep repeating the same arguments to him.

5. LOOK AT ME AND BE ASTONISHED: Job is still bewildered as to why these men, who call themselves his friends, have so far failed to show him any compassion.

7. WHY DO THE WICKED LIVE AND BECOME OLD: Job denies Bildad's claim that the wicked die young and have no offspring to remember them. In fact, the wicked often go peacefully to their graves. Solomon would later anguish over this same point (see Ecclesiastes 8:10).

16. **INDEED THEIR PROSPERITY IS NOT IN THEIR HAND**: Job acknowledges that this prospering by the wicked is not of their own doing, but is allowed to happen by God.

17. **HOW OFTEN IS THE LAMP OF THE WICKED PUT OUT?** Job plays off Bildad's sentiments (see 18:5–6, 18–19) to refute each of his assertions about the judgment of sinners.

22. **CAN ANYONE TEACH GOD KNOWLEDGE**: Job suggests here that his friends are guilty of telling God how He must deal with people.

23. **ONE DIES IN HIS FULL STRENGTH**: Some of the wicked live and die in prosperity, but others do not, which cancels out the absolutist nature of his friend's argument.

28. **YOU SAY, "WHERE IS THE HOUSE OF THE PRINCE?"** Again, Job refers to the statements of his friends (Zophar in this case; see 20:7), who are trying to prove "sin equals suffering."

29. **HAVE YOU NOT ASKED THOSE WHO TRAVEL THE ROAD** Job knows his friends will not listen to him. So he suggests they ask travelers, any of whom will tell them that wicked people sometimes prosper in this life. Yet there will be a day of doom for them when they die.

34. **EMPTY WORDS**: The boastful words of the counselors were contradicted by facts.

UNLEASHING THE TEXT

1) According to Bildad, what are the root causes of the suffering experienced by wicked people?

2) How do money and wealth factor into the arguments of Bildad and Zophar?

3) Where do you see evidence of Job's faith in God throughout his responses to Bildad and Zophar?

_____

_____

_____

_____

4) What did Job mean when he spoke of his Redeemer? What did he believe this Redeemer would do for him?

_____

_____

_____

_____

EXPLORING THE MEANING

Actions have consequences. In continuing to argue that evil people receive punishment for their evil actions, Bildad and Zophar emphasize a true principle—that actions have consequences. Specifically, those who disobey God or seek to do what is wrong suffer the harmful effects of their actions. As Paul wrote, "If you do evil, be afraid" (Romans 13:4).

Bildad said, "The light of the wicked indeed goes out . . . for he is cast into a net by his own feet, and he walks into a snare. The net takes him by the heel, and a snare lays hold of him" (Job 18:5, 8–9). In other words, those who scheme and plot in an effort to take advantage of others are often caught in the same kinds of traps they love to set—and this often leads to their downfall. Zophar expressed this idea with powerful imagery: "Though evil is sweet in his mouth, and he hides it under his tongue . . . yet his food in his stomach turns sour; it becomes cobra venom within him. He swallows down riches and vomits them up again" (20:12, 14–15).

Solomon used language similar to Bildad and Zophar when he said, "Whoever digs a pit will fall into it, and he who rolls a stone will have it roll back on him" (Proverbs 26:27). It is true that lying, cheating, and other sins often lead to punishments when those who perpetrate such acts are exposed. The problem is that Job's companions kept pushing the notion that evil will *always* be punished, and tragedies are *always* the result of sin. Real life is more complicated.

In addition, Bildad and Zophar were correct to point out that those who make wealth and possessions the primary pursuit of their lives are disappointed—especially when they trample on the poor to pad their own pockets. In the end, money really does not buy happiness. As Jesus said, "Do not lay up for yourselves treasures on earth, where moth and rust destroy and where thieves break in and steal; but lay up for yourselves treasures in heaven, where neither moth nor rust destroys" (Matthew 6:19–20).

History provides perspective for our choices: One other principle that Bildad and Zophar mentioned in their respective arguments is that people who make evil choices and revel in injustice are often judged harshly in the broader perspective of history. Zophar claimed that "the triumphing of the wicked is short, and the joy of the hypocrite is but for a moment" (20:5). Bildad added of such a person, "His roots are dried out below, and his branch withers above. The memory of him perishes from the earth, and he has no name among the renowned. He is driven from light into darkness, and chased out of the world" (Job 18:16–18).

On the other hand, the deeds of the righteous are remembered for generations. Solomon wrote, "A good man leaves an inheritance to his children's children, but the wealth of the sinner is stored up for the righteous" (Proverbs 13:22). King David, commenting on the deeds of God, wrote, "One generation shall praise Your works to another, and shall declare Your mighty acts. . . . Men shall speak of the might of Your awesome acts, and I will declare Your greatness. They shall utter the memory of Your great goodness" (Psalm 145:4, 6–7).

Job's companions were thus correct in pointing out that those who choose to invest in wickedness never escape judgment. As Scripture says, "Be sure your sin will find you out" (Numbers 32:23).

Our Redeemer lives! In the midst of Job's response to Bildad and Zophar, he makes an incredible declaration of faith: "For I know that my Redeemer lives, and He shall stand at last on the earth; and after my skin is destroyed, this I know, that in my flesh I shall see God" (Job 19:25–26). These words are striking for many reasons, one of which is that Job spoke them in the midst of his intense sorrow and despair.

In Hebrew culture, a redeemer was someone—typically a family member—who was willing to pay a price in order to secure another's freedom. For instance, if someone had been forced to sell their home in order to pay a debt, a family member could step in and redeem that property by essentially purchasing it back for the original owner.

In one sense, then, Job was expressing confidence that God would eventually step in on his behalf and "redeem" his integrity. Eliphaz, Bildad, and Zophar had continually proclaimed him to be guilty of great sin against God. But Job fully believed that God Himself would intervene to vindicate him and declare him free of any wrongdoing.

More importantly, Job's words are a powerful prophecy that point to Jesus and the gospel. By willingly offering Himself as a sacrifice on the cross, Jesus paid the price for the sin of those who will be saved, and He redeemed them through His blood. Job was correct that his Redeemer lives and would "stand at last on the earth." Those promises were ultimately fulfilled in Christ.

REFLECTING ON THE TEXT

5) When have you recently experienced the truth that actions have consequences?

_____

_____

_____

_____

_____

6) Why is it critical to avoid the trap of possessions and wealth in today's society?

_____

_____

_____

_____

7) How have you personally benefitted from Jesus' role as Redeemer?

_____

_____

_____

_____

8) Why is it important to recognize that Job's words pointed forward to Jesus, even though Job himself did not understand the future role of the Messiah?

_____

_____

_____

_____

PERSONAL RESPONSE

9) How will your family view your life when they view it through the perspective of history? How do you *want* them to view your life when your days in this world are over?

_____

_____

_____

_____

10) In what ways should Jesus' role as your Redeemer influence your actions and attitudes throughout this week?

_____

_____

_____

_____

_____

6

AN ACCUSATION OF WICKEDNESS
Job 22:1–24:25

DRAWING NEAR
How do you typically respond when you face tragedy or loss?

_____

_____

_____

_____

_____

_____

THE CONTEXT
Like combatants on a carousel, Job and his companions once again go round and round on the subject of sin and suffering and righteousness and reward. As with the previous two cycles, Eliphaz begins this third round of arguments. This time, it is clear that his frustration with Job has reached a new level. He abandons any pretense of civility and directly accuses Job of engaging in wickedness. Perhaps he hopes this more direct assault will get through to Job.

Eliphaz's theme is the same as in his previous discourses—his worldview allows no deviation from his preconceived ideas of how the moral order of the universe functions. In his eyes, Job is simply being punished by God for his sin. If Job truly desires to be free from his suffering, as he has claimed, he must repent so that he can be restored to God's blessing.

For his part, Job's discourses in this third cycle seem to ignore the arguments of both Eliphaz and Bildad. (Zophar does not participate.) Instead, Job speaks more often and more directly to God. Increasingly, he appeals to God and asks for an opportunity to make his case—to clarify the evidence of his life and confirm that he has maintained his integrity.

KEYS TO THE TEXT

Read Job 22:1–24:25, noting the key words and phrases indicated below.

> A PAINFUL ACCUSATION: *Eliphaz, growing more and more frustrated with Job's refusal to listen to their arguments, accuses Job of outright wickedness.*

22:2 CAN A MAN BE PROFITABLE TO GOD: Eliphaz is the least vindictive of Job's counselors, but as his frustration rises, even he gets nasty with Job at this point. He bypasses Job's previous statements and accuses him of various sins and of failing to appreciate the attributes of God.

3. IS IT ANY PLEASURE TO THE ALMIGHTY THAT YOU ARE RIGHTEOUS? The Hebrew in this section of Job is difficult, but Eliphaz is evidently emphasizing the almighty nature of God, saying that God is so lofty and transcendent that He has no direct concern at all with Job, doesn't care about his complaints and claims to righteousness, and is not involved in the trivia of Job's life.

4. IS IT BECAUSE OF YOUR FEAR: Eliphaz no longer believes that Job is a God-fearing man. The fact that his troubles are so great testify to Eliphaz the extent of Job's sin.

5. IS NOT YOUR WICKEDNESS GREAT: This miserable comforter accuses Job of wickedness that is great, naming various sins against humanity as the reasons for Job's trouble.

6. YOU HAVE TAKEN PLEDGES FROM YOUR BROTHER: Eliphaz describes Job's sins in terms of social oppression and neglect. He believes that Job has deceived himself by trusting in his own righteousness while failing to do good to other people.

10. SNARES ARE ALL AROUND: The consequences of Job's supposed sins are snares, perils, darkness, and floods. These are not meant in a literal sense but were commonly used in the Old Testament as symbols of trouble (see Psalm 42:7; 91:3–6; Isaiah 8:7, 22; 43:2).

15–16. WICKED MEN . . . CUT DOWN BEFORE THEIR TIME: Again, Eliphaz expresses the fate of the wicked using the simplistic idea that all suffering is the direct result of sin. Contrary to what Job has argued, Eliphaz holds to the belief that the wicked characteristically die prematurely.

20. SURELY OUR ADVERSARIES ARE CUT DOWN: Eliphaz again flatly rejects Job's claim that God allows the wicked to prosper.

21. ACQUAINT YOURSELF WITH HIM: Eliphaz paints a picture of the life of blessing in store for Job if only he will return to God and repent of his sin.

24. YOU WILL LAY YOUR GOLD IN THE DUST: Eliphaz implies that Job needs to turn from his love of wealth to a love of God. This charge was patently not true, as Job has already made clear his desire to see God (see 19:25–27). Eliphaz and the others were likely taken back by Job's honest words of frustration to God, which to them served as "proof" that Job needed to repent.

OPHIR: A land with high-quality gold, whose location is uncertain (see Genesis 10:29).

30. HE WILL EVEN DELIVER ONE WHO IS NOT INNOCENT: This closing statement emphasizes the fact that Eliphaz does *not* believe Job was innocent. His line of reasoning appears to be, "Stop all the speeches and complaints, repent, and everything will be fine."

A LONGING FOR FELLOWSHIP: In the middle of tragedy, and beset by horrible counselors, Job expresses his desire for God to intervene.

23:2. EVEN TODAY MY COMPLAINT IS BITTER: Job's tone in this section indicates that he had moved from reacting to his friends' accusations to contemplating his own condition before God.

3. TO HIS SEAT: A place of God's judgment.

4. PRESENT MY CASE: Job's claim to innocence.

6. WOULD HE CONTEND WITH ME: Job knows that God is not going to enter a contest with him to determine, as in a court case, who is right. But he wants God to at least listen to him! He is confident that he could make his case and be delivered by his just Judge.

7. THERE THE UPRIGHT COULD REASON WITH HIM: Job reasserts his claim to be an upright man with renewed confidence that God would agree with him. He is certain the outcome would be positive if only he could gain an audience with God. At first glance this might seem like pride, but we have seen that Job's life was so rooted in the fear of God that even the Lord held him up as an example of godliness. King David did the same: "Let my vindication come from Your presence; let Your eyes look on the things that are upright. You have tested my heart; You have visited me in the night; You have tried me and have found nothing" (Psalm 17:2–3).

8. HE IS NOT THERE: Even though Job cannot sense God's presence, he believes that the Lord is present. He affirms his commitment to God's purpose in this test.

10. HE HAS TESTED ME: Job does not think God is testing him as a means of revealing his sin but to prove that he will come through the ordeal as pure gold.

11. MY FOOT HAS HELD FAST TO HIS STEPS: Job commits his continued obedience to God's Word and promises not to depart from the Lord's commandments.

14. HE PERFORMS WHAT IS APPOINTED FOR ME: Job's confidence in God's sovereignty faltered at times in practice, but he returned to it repeatedly. This is the great lesson of the book: *Trust in the sovereign God even when you cannot understand why things go badly in life.*

15. I AM TERRIFIED AT HIS PRESENCE: Job's fear is natural in light of his recognition that God is unique and cannot be told what to do by human beings.

JOB'S COMPLAINT: *Job concludes by listing the kinds of severe sins that go on in the world that seem to go unpunished by God.*

24:1. TIMES ARE NOT HIDDEN: Job believes that God knows the appointed times for all activities under the sun. As Solomon wrote, "To everything there is a season, a time for every purpose under heaven" (Ecclesiastes 3:1). Yet Job bemoans the fact that God does not inform humans about these appointed seasons.

2. REMOVE LANDMARKS: Job has made the point that the unrighteous prosper in spite of their sins. Extending that theme, he now lists the kinds of severe sins which go on in the world that God doesn't seem to punish. The ancient practice of removing landmarks is addressed in Deuteronomy 19:14: "You shall not remove your neighbor's landmark, which the men of old have set." Corrupt landowners did this to increase their holdings, particularly where the land was owned by bereaved widows.

3. THEY TAKE THE WIDOW'S OX: Taking advantage of widows will be treated by the ultimate court in heaven. The sins that Job names here—oppressing the orphans, widows, and poor, and committing murder, thievery, and adultery—are forbidden in other parts of the Old Testament.

7. SPEND THE NIGHT: It was common practice to take an outer garment as a pledge for money owed. However, the Old Testament law forbade keeping the garment at night, as its owner could get cold and sick. "If the man is poor, you shall not keep his pledge overnight. You shall in any case return the pledge to him again when the sun goes down, that he may sleep in his own garment and bless you" (Deuteronomy 24:12–13).

12. YET GOD DOES NOT CHARGE THEM WITH WRONG: This is a stinging accusation from Job. Human courts prosecuted offenders for most of these social crimes. Job, in essence, is saying, "If human courts punish the wicked, then why doesn't God?"

14–17. THEY DO NOT KNOW THE LIGHT: The murderer, the adulterer, and the thief all share the trait of loving the darkness rather than the light. As Jesus said, "Everyone practicing evil hates the light and does not come to the light, lest his deeds should be exposed" (John 3:20).

18. THEIR PORTION SHOULD BE CURSED IN THE EARTH: Job again refers to the opinions of his counselors, saying that if their view is correct, all the wicked should be experiencing punishment (they should all be "cursed in the earth"). But it is obvious they are not.

24. THEY ARE EXALTED FOR A LITTLE WHILE: Job's view is that the punishment of the wicked will come *eventually*. Retribution needs the timing of God's wisdom—when He determines the wrongs that will be made right. Job is confident that this point could not be refuted.

UNLEASHING THE TEXT

1) What was the point of Eliphaz's barrage of rhetorical questions in Job 22? What was the primary point he was trying to make?

_____

_____

_____

_____

_____

2) How would you summarize Job's view of God in Job 23–24?

_____

_____

_____

_____

3) What are some of the ways Job expressed his longing to reconnect with God?

_____

_____

_____

_____

4) What atrocities did Job mention in Job 24 that seemingly go unpunished by God?

_____

_____

_____

_____

EXPLORING THE MEANING

There is value in repentance. In his third speech, Eliphaz is particularly insulting to Job, labeling him as a man of great "wickedness" and "iniquity without end" (22:5). He accuses Job of stripping poor people of their clothes, withholding food from the hungry, refusing to help widows, and more. His goal, as before, is to push Job toward repentance.

In speaking on this subject, Eliphaz correctly and even eloquently describes the benefits of coming before God to repent of our sin. "If you return to the Almighty, you will be built up," he states. "You will remove iniquity far from your tents" (verse 23). He adds, "For then you will have your delight in the Almighty, and lift up your face to God. You will make your prayer to Him, He will hear you, and you will pay your vows" (verses 26–27).

In spite of Eliphaz's flaws as a comforter, uplifting the benefits of repentance is a thoroughly biblical principle. In fact, Jesus began His public ministry by proclaiming, "Repent, for the kingdom of heaven is at hand" (Matthew 4:17). The apostle Peter urged, "Repent therefore and be converted, that your sins may be blotted out, so that times of refreshing may come from the presence of the Lord" (Acts 3:19). The Bible is filled with the stories of people like David who honestly repented of their sin and were restored to fellowship with God.

In short, we are all guilty of disobedience to God's commands. But when we sin, we can confidently take Eliphaz's advice and come before God's throne to repent. As the author of Hebrews stated, "Let us therefore come boldly to the throne of grace, that we may obtain mercy and find grace to help in time of need" (Hebrews 4:16). God will welcome us when we take such action, and He has already made provision for our forgiveness.

There is value in fearing God. Job frequently describes God's nature and character throughout his conversations and arguments with his three friends. For example, in Job 23, he refers to God's "great power" and notes that "the upright could reason with Him" (verses 6–7). Despite Job's suffering, he treasured God's words "more than my necessary food" (verse 12).

But then Job makes this statement: "I am terrified at His presence . . . I am afraid of Him. For God made my heart weak, and the Almighty terrifies me" (verses 15–16). If this seems surprising to you, it is likely because Christians today (rightly) emphasize a personal relationship with God, available to us through Christ. We think of God as both our Friend and our heavenly Father. Paul wrote, "You did not receive the spirit of bondage again to fear, but you received the Spirit of adoption by whom we cry out, 'Abba, Father'" (Romans 8:15).

However, throughout much of the Bible, we see that people who encounter God primarily react with fear. For instance, here is how the Israelites responded to God's presence when Moses received the Ten Commandments: "Now all the people witnessed the thunderings, the lightning flashes, the sound of the trumpet, and the mountain smoking; and when the people saw *it*, they trembled and stood afar off. Then they said to Moses, 'You speak with us, and we will hear; but let not God speak with us, lest we die'" (Exodus 20:18–19). When Peter first began to realize who Jesus is, "he fell down at Jesus' knees, saying, 'Depart from me, for I am a sinful man, O Lord!'"

There is value in such fear. It's not a craven fear. We don't need to be afraid of God in the same way we are afraid of darkness or dangerous animals. God does not seek to harm us. However, we benefit when we have a proper respect for God's power and His holiness. It was for this reason that Solomon wrote, "The fear of the LORD is the beginning of knowledge" (Proverbs 1:7).

Evil is a real and present danger in this world. Eliphaz had accused Job of heinous crimes. Job does not respond by defending himself or attempting to deny those accusations. Instead, he turns Eliphaz's words against him by highlighting the reality that evil people *do* exist in the world. Job spends much of chapter 24 highlighting these acts of evil. His point is simple: If people commit these acts without receiving punishment from God, why was it so hard to believe that Job could experience suffering without it being a punishment?

As a byproduct of Job's argument, it is important to note that evil *does* have a place in our world. Job was correct in observing that powerful people choose to "snatch the fatherless from the breast, and take a pledge from the poor. They cause the poor to go naked, without clothing; and they take away the sheaves from the hungry" (24:9–10). Job highlights the injustice of poor laborers who work all day to pad the pockets of the wealthy. He notes the wickedness of adulterers, thieves, and others who choose to live in darkness.

It is easy to throw blame at God for the existence of such evil. After all, we reason, He could prevent such wickedness if He determined to do so. In truth, the fact that evil is part of our world is proof that God has a purpose for it. And we know that His purposes are always good. He can use even the detestable fruits of evil for good. Indeed, the most wicked deed in the history of the universe—the crucifixion of the sinless Son of God—resulted in the salvation of countless sinners. God constantly glorifies Himself by making all things, including eveil, work together for good (see Romans 8:28). And one day His glory will be exalted by the utter destruction of evil and its final elimination from the universe. In the meantime, we maintain our trust in both His goodness and His sovereignty.

REFLECTING ON THE TEXT

5) What do you consider to be the distinguishing marks of authentic repentance?

-----

6) How would you summarize what it means to fear the Lord in your daily life?

_____

_____

_____

_____

7) In what way do you tend to view God: as harsh Judge or loving Father? Explain.

_____

_____

_____

_____

8) As people created by God and accountable to him, what should our attitude be toward evil in this world?

_____

_____

_____

_____

PERSONAL RESPONSE

9) Where is there a need for repentance in your life?

_____

_____

_____

_____

10) How can you incorporate fear or awe into your relationship with God?

_____

_____

_____

_____

7

A Discourse on Human Frailty

Job 25:1–26:14

Drawing Near

What features of the natural world tend to remind you of God's glory? Why?

_____

_____

_____

_____

_____

_____

_____

The Context

Job has endured a grueling three-round verbal duel with his companions Eliphaz, Bildad, and Zophar. In Job 25–26, we come to an end of these conversations, with Bildad again making the point that God is righteous and should not be questioned by humans. In truth, Bildad has little to add to his previous arguments, summing up his statements in this round in just six verses.

The point that Bildad chooses to emphasize in these final comments is on God's transcendence and dominion over the moral order. His goal is to reiterate his point on the fallen state of humanity—even calling human beings "maggots" and "worms" (verse 6). This is a strikingly different picture from one we find in the opening chapter of Genesis, where we read God saying, "Let Us make man in Our image, according to Our likeness" (1:26). Job, for his part, concludes by extolling God's majesty and human frailty.

By the end of Job 26, we are more than halfway through the book. The next phases will include a series of monologues from Job, in addition to another conversation with a younger man named Elihu. Finally, the book concludes with God Himself stepping in to put an end to the discussion once and for all—and then restoring Job's possessions and blessing him for his faithfulnes.

KEYS TO THE TEXT

Read Job 25:1–26:14, noting the key words and phrases indicated below.

FINAL WORDS: Bildad gives his third and final discourse—the last speech made by Job's friends—and restates his theory that God is majestic and humanity is sinful.

25:1. BILDAD THE SHUHITE ANSWERED: Bildad's closing argument to Job is short in nature. He does not choose to answer Job's most recent argument—or even bother to present a new one of his own making—but simply offers a brief statement in which he basically repeats all that has been said previously by Eliphaz (see, for example, Job 4:17–21; 15:14–16).

2. DOMINION AND FEAR BELONG TO HIM: Bildad wants to show that God is pure and has complete dominion over the moral order in order to prove the impurity of humans (and, by extension, the impurity and sin in Job).

4–5. HOW THEN CAN MAN BE RIGHTEOUS BEFORE GOD? Bildad notes that God's majesty is above everything in this universe, including the moon and stars. No person can be considered righteous in God's eyes. As God later said through the prophet Isaiah, "All we like sheep have gone astray; we have turned, every one, to his own way" (53:6).

6. MAN, WHO IS A MAGGOT: This is Bildad's main point in citing his reflections on God's supreme righteousness and majesty—that humans are all "maggots" when compared to the holiness of God. The apostle Paul later wrote that the Law of God revealed "all have sinned and fall short of the glory of God" (Romans 3:23). However, he added, "Where sin abounded, grace abounded much more, so that as sin reigned in death, even so grace might reign through righteousness to eternal life through Jesus Christ our Lord" (5:20–21). When we are saved through faith in Jesus' completed work on the cross, we become "children . . . heirs of God and joint heirs with Christ" (8:17). God sees us not as maggots or worms but as His beloved sons and daughters!

> JOB'S FINAL REBUTTAL: *Job responds to Bildad, showing that his theological and rational words missed the point of his need altogether and have been no help.*

26.2. HOW HAVE YOU HELPED HIM WHO IS WITHOUT POWER? As we have seen, Job's friends have been striving to make the point that Job's suffering came about as a result of sin in his life. Job has steadfastly argued against this claim, stating his desire to "speak to the Almighty" and "defend [his] own ways before Him" (13:3, 15). Job is determined to be vindicated, while Bildad has basically stated that such vindication before God is impossible.

3. AND HOW HAVE YOU DECLARED SOUND ADVICE TO MANY? Job sarcastically challenges Bildad's "wisdom" in this matter, asking how he has really helped anyone.

4. TO WHOM HAVE YOU UTTERED WORDS? This can also be rendered, "With whose help have you uttered words?" (as in the *English Standard Version*). Job wants to know the source from which Bildad is pulling his supposed wisdom. Certainly, he knows that Bildad is repeating Eliphaz's arguments. Job is angered at this point because all his friends are viewing him as a reprehensible sinner. In Bildad's words, he is just a "worm" whose case before God is utterly hopeless. Job's retort is that they are equally hopeless as counselors.

5. THE DEAD TREMBLE: As before, Job reveals that he is not inferior to his friends in describing God's greatness (see Job 9 and 12). Job's theme here is similar to that of Bildad—that God has vast power—but he comes to a different conclusion. Bildad reduced humanity to the status of worms—depraved and hopeless. But Job refutes the concept that God's transcendant power itself rules out human reconciliation with their Creator.

6. SHEOL . . . DESTRUCTION: The realm of the dead. "Hell and Destruction are before the LORD; so how much more the hearts of the sons of men" (Proverbs 15:11).

7. HANGS THE EARTH ON NOTHING: A statement that is accurate, given in ancient time before scientific verification. This indicates the divine authorship of Scripture.

8. HE BINDS UP THE WATER IN HIS THICK CLOUDS: The clouds in the sky contain an immense quantity of water, yet they do not split and dump out all the water at once. Job's language in this section highlights the incredible and mysterious power of God.

9. HE COVERS THE FACE OF HIS THRONE: God uses the clouds to enshroud the glory of His heavenly throng. "He who builds His layers in the sky, and has founded His strata in the earth; who calls for the waters of the sea, and pours them out on the face of the earth—the LORD is His name" (Amos 9:6).

10. A CIRCULAR HORIZON: This describes the Earth as a globe, which is another scientifically accurate statement at a time when many people thought the world was flat.

11. PILLARS OF HEAVEN: A figure of speech for the mountains that seem to hold up the sky. "He looks on the earth, and it trembles; He touches the hills, and they smoke" (Psalm 104:32).

12. BREAKS UP THE STORM: Literally, "Rahab" (see Job 9:13; Isaiah 51:9). This term seems to be widely used to describe various things that wreak havoc.

13. HIS SPIRIT: The Holy Spirit worked mightily in creation. "The earth was without form, and void; and darkness was on the face of the deep. And the Spirit of God was hovering over the face of the waters" (Genesis 1:2).

THE FLEEING SERPENT: This is figurative language for the idea that God brought all constellations into subjection under His authority. The word "serpent" could be translated "crooked" and refer to any wayward stars or planets being brought under control by God's mighty power.

14. INDEED THESE ARE THE MERE EDGES OF HIS WAYS: Both Job and Bildad deal with the cosmos and the majesty of God. However, Job ends on a note of human wonder and hope in this mysterious God of the universe, rather than viewing all humanity as worms and maggots before Him. Job thus employs his poetic language to remind his counselors that all that could be said and understood by humans was a mere glimpse of God's powerful hand.

UNLEASHING THE TEXT

1) Where do you see evidence of humanity's weakness and frailty?

----

2) Where do you see evidence of God's greatness and majesty displayed in the
world today?

_____

_____

_____

_____

_____

3) What was Job trying to communicate through his use of rhetorical questions
at the beginning of chapter 26?

_____

_____

_____

_____

_____

4) Which images caught your attention most in chapter 26? Why?

_____

_____

_____

_____

_____

EXPLORING THE MEANING

The reality of human frailty. In Bildad's brief final speech, he addresses the truth
that human beings are unworthy of standing before a holy God. After proclaiming God's majesty, Bildad asks, "How then can man be righteous before God?
Or how can he be pure who is born of a woman?" (25:4). He notes that something as great as the moon only reflects light, and the stars in the heavens are not
pure in comparison to God. Therefore, "How much less man, who is a maggot,
and a son of man, who is a worm?" (verse 6). These are strong images, but they
effectively communicate the idea that humanity is insignificant before God.

Job also addresses the weakness of humanity, but from a different angle.
"How have you helped him who is without power?" he asks Bildad—and,
by extension, Eliphaz and Zophar. "How have you saved the arm that has

no strength? How have you counseled one who has no wisdom? And how have you declared sound advice to many?" (26:1–3). In short, Job agreed that human beings are weak, yet he wants to know what his companions have done to help those who are frail and in need of assistance. All three of his friends have failed to support God's work by serving others, just as they had failed to comfort him in his time of suffering.

It should be noted that humanity's fragility in comparison with God does not mean that human beings have little value in God's eyes. Quite the opposite— David writes that we have been "fearfully and wonderfully made" (Psalm 139:14). Paul writes that God "chose us in Him before the foundation of the world, that we should be holy and without blame before Him in love" (Ephesians 1:4). Every man and woman has been created in God's image, which means every person who ever has and ever will live carries an intrinsic value. But God's image in man has been marred by sin. So God made a way to redeem repentant sinners through the sacrifice that Christ made on the cross.

The reality of God's greatness. Bildad begins his final speech by extolling the greatness of God: "Dominion and fear belong to Him; He makes peace in His high places. Is there any number to His armies? Upon whom does His light not rise?" (25:2–3). His point throughout the discourse has been that God is far above all created things, which means He cannot be questioned or called to account by any created thing—let alone a man, who is a "worm" or "maggot."

Job responds to Bildad by waxing eloquent on God's power: "The dead tremble, those under the waters and those inhabiting them. Sheol is naked before Him, and Destruction has no covering" (26:5–6). Job rightly claims that God is above not only created things, but also the forces of death, destruction, and the afterlife. Just as importantly, Job enumerates some of the ways that God's greatness can be witnessed and understood through creation. He speaks of God binding up the clouds with water, drawing "a circular horizon on the face of the waters" (verse 10), and even hanging the earth "on nothing" (verse 7)—a surprising insight given the lack of scientific understanding of planets and outer space in Job's day.

In making these observations, Job confirms what the apostle Paul would later write to the church in Rome: "For since the creation of the world His invisible attributes are clearly seen, being understood by the things that are made, even His eternal power and Godhead, so that they are without excuse" (Romans 1:20).

REFLECTING ON THE TEXT

5) Is it right or wrong for humans to question God's actions or motives? Explain.

6) How do you understand the truth that you are created in God's image? How does that truth influence your everyday life?

7) When has an encounter in nature helped you catch a picture or a glimpse of God's greatness?

8) Why is it important for Christians to have a firm grasp on science and a good understanding of the natural world?

PERSONAL RESPONSE

9) Where do you have opportunities this week to help someone who is in need?

10) How do you see the glory of God on display in creation? How does that inform your worship and praise?

_____

_____

_____

_____

_____

8

JOB DEFENDS HIS INTEGRITY

Job 27:1–31:40

DRAWING NEAR
How would you respond if your integrity came under attack as Job's did?

_____

_____

_____

_____

_____

_____

_____

THE CONTEXT
The central issue in the argument between Job and his companions was the source of Job's suffering, which included the loss of his family, his wealth, and even his health. Eliphaz, Bildad, and Zophar followed the conventional wisdom of their day, which said that God punished wrongdoing and blessed righteousness. Therefore, they believed strongly that Job must have sinned greatly in order to receive such a stunning blow as punishment.

Job, however, knew that he had not rebelled against God. He understood himself to be a sinner and someone who had fallen short of the divine standard, yet he was firm in his stance that he had not intentionally departed from God's will or His statutes. Having finished three cycles of discourse with his companions, he now engaged in two monologues to further clarify his point and support his claims. In the first, he again declares his integrity. In the second, he reflects on his earlier life—and his earlier connection with God—and reaffirms his appeal to heaven for justice.

KEYS TO THE TEXT

Read Job 27:1–31:40, noting the key words and phrases indicated below.

> *JOB'S FIRST MONOLOGUE: No longer arguing with his three companions, Job defends his righteousness to any who will listen.*

27:2 WHO HAS TAKEN AWAY MY JUSTICE: God did not speak to declare Job innocent. The same was true of Christ: "In His humiliation His justice was taken away" (Acts 8:33).

4. MY LIPS WILL NOT SPEAK WICKEDNESS: Job affirms his true and stead-fast devotion to righteous living, no matter what happens to him. He refuses to live with a guilty conscience. This was no brash claim, for God had also recognized Job's virtue (see 1:8; 2:3).

7. MAY MY ENEMY BE LIKE THE WICKED: Job may here be calling for God to judge his accusers as He judges the wicked.

8. WHAT IS THE HOPE OF THE HYPOCRITE: Job reminds his friends that he will never be hypocritical because he understands the dire consequences.

11. I WILL TEACH YOU ABOUT THE HAND OF GOD: Job and his friends all agreed that God was powerful, wise, and sovereign. However, because Job knew there was no cherished sin in his life that would bring about the intense suffering he was enduring, he was forced to conclude that the simplistic notion that all suffering comes from sin, and that all righteousness is rewarded, is wrong. At the outset, Job probably believed as the comforters did, but he had seen that his friends' limitation of God's action was in need of revision. In fact, it was nonsense. Job's immediate comments introduce his exposition on wisdom that will soon follow (see Job 28).

13. THIS IS THE PORTION OF A WICKED MAN WITH GOD: Job wants it made clear that he is not denying that the wicked are punished with severe distress. In this section, he agrees with his friends that the wicked do, indeed, suffer greatly. However, he contentds, this reality explains nothing in his particular case, since he is righteous.

18. HOUSE LIKE A MOTH, LIKE A BOOTH: These are temporary dwellings, which illustrate that the wicked will not live long.

23. CLAP THEIR HANDS: A gesture of mocking.

SUPERNATURAL WISDOM: Job calls on his friends to consider that perhaps God's wisdom is beyond their comprehension.

28.1–2. A MINE FOR SILVER . . . GOLD . . . IRON . . . COPPER: Humans expend tremendous effort in securing these precious metals from the earth.

3. MAN PUTS AN END TO DARKNESS: Archaeology reveals that ancient miners often "[put] an end to darkness" by cutting shafts to the mines to let in sunlight. These types of shafts are seen in the elaborate underground waterways in cities such as Jerusalem and Megiddo. Mining lamps were also used in gold mining in Nubia (located in Egypt) during the first century BC.

5. UNDERNEATH IT IS TURNED UP AS BY FIRE: Possibly a reference to volcanic action, though there is evidence that ancient miners used fire to split rock and reach the ore.

12. BUT WHERE CAN WISDOM BE FOUND? This verse sums up the message of the chapter. The point is that no amount of effort, even effort as vigorous and demanding as mining, will yield God's wisdom. It is not gained by natural or theoretical knowledge, but only by the sovereign will of God. What God does not reveal, humans cannot hope to know.

21. IT IS HIDDEN FROM THE EYES OF ALL LIVING: While human intellect and ingenuity have enabled people to accomplish great feats, they cannot secure God's wisdom on their own. That treasure, greater than any precious metal or gemstone, comes only by the revelation of God Himself.

22. DESTRUCTION AND DEATH: Those who reach this place will have a belated understanding that they missed God's wisdom in life (see Luke 16:19–31). But even though they now see their folly, they still fall short of genuine wisdom. Thus, "Destruction and Death" are personified in this verse in order to testify that in that dark realm where the wicked go after death, wisdom is known only by reputation.

23. GOD UNDERSTANDS ITS WAY, AND HE KNOWS ITS PLACE: These are perhaps the most important thoughts in the chapter for the debates. Job and his friends have probed God's wisdom three times and, basically, have arrived nowhere near the truth. Finally, Job makes the point that the divine wisdom necessary to explain his suffering is inaccessible to humans. Only God knows it, because only He knows everything.

26. WHEN HE MADE A LAW: True wisdom belongs to the One who is the Almighty Creator of the universe. People can only know such wisdom if God declares it to them.

28. BEHOLD, THE FEAR OF THE LORD, THAT IS WISDOM: Job had made the connection the others would not. While the specific features of God's wisdom may not be revealed to us, the alpha and omega of wisdom is to revere God and avoid sin, leaving the unanswered questions to Him in trusting submission. All a person can do is trust and obey. "Let us hear the conclusion of the whole matter: Fear God and keep His commandments, for this is man's all" (Ecclesiastes 12:13).

JOB'S SECOND MONOLOGUE: *Job laments the totality of his fall, yet he still maintains his righteousness and integrity.*

29:2. OH, THAT I WERE AS IN MONTHS PAST: Job does not change his mind about his sin. He continues to deny that he earned the pain that he is enduring through personal iniquity. The realities of his own words in the previous chapter have not yet fully taken over his mind, so here he swings back to despair and rehearses what his life was like before all this calamity had befallen him.

5. WHEN THE ALMIGHTY WAS YET WITH ME: Before these tumultuous events struck, Job had felt fulfilled because God was with him. The Lord was now still present with Job, but to him it felt as if God had abandoned him. Yet God would soon demonstrate to Job, by addressing his criticisms, that He has been with him throughout this ordeal.

6. BATHED WITH CREAM . . . RIVERS OF OIL: Job had once had the richest milk and best olive oil in abundance.

7. TOOK MY SEAT IN THE OPEN SQUARE: This was a place in society reserved for city leaders. Job had been one because he was a wealthy and powerful man.

12–13. I DELIVERED THE POOR: In the ancient Near Eastern world, a man's virtue was measured by his treatment of the weakest and most vulnerable members of society. If he protected and provided for this group, he was respected as being a noble man. Job's accusers claimed that he must have not done these things, otherwise he wouldn't have been suffering (see 22:1–11).

15. I WAS EYES TO THE BLIND: Contrary to the accusations of his friends, Job went beyond the standards of the day to care for the widow, the orphan, the poor, the disabled, and the abused.

16. I SEARCHED OUT THE CASE: Much oppression occurred in unjust courts, but there Job protected the weak.

18. I SHALL DIE IN MY NEST: Job had vigorous health like a widely rooted tree enjoying fresh dew (see verse 19), and he had expected to live a long life with his family (in his "nest").

21. MEN LISTENED TO ME: Job reminds his friends that there had been a day when no one rejected his insights. He was the one people sought for counsel.

24. IF I MOCKED: This is likely a reference to saying something facetiously or jokingly. Job's word was so respected that they didn't believe his humor was humor, but took it seriously.

25. DWELT AS A KING: Job was not a king but a high local official, such as a mayor. Mayors, called *hazannu* in Job's day, performed all of the activities Job claimed in the previous section.

LOSS OF DIGNITY: Job expands on his theme and stresses the degree to which he has lost his dignity and respect among the members of his society.

30:1. PUT WITH THE DOGS: Job describes his mockers as dissipated vagabonds who, because of their uselessness and wickedness, were not welcome in society, so were driven out of the land. These base men had now made Job the object of their sordid entertainment.

9. I AM THEIR TAUNTING SONG: In former days, Job would not even hire these mockers' fathers to tend his animals like sheepdogs. Now, he was the object of their jeering.

16–19. THE DAYS OF AFFLICTION TAKE HOLD: Job's life is ebbing away, suffering has gripped him, his bones ache, his gnawing pain never relents, his skin ("garment") is disfigured (see verse 30), and he has been reduced to mud, dirt, and ashes.

20. YOU DO NOT ANSWER ME: This caused Job the most suffering of all—what seemed to be the cruel silence of God.

23. THE HOUSE APPOINTED: The grave.

24. SURELY HE WOULD NOT STRETCH OUT HIS HAND: Job here is saying that God, like himself, must have some sympathy so as not to altogether destroy what is already ruined. Job had believed that truth, and reached out for help in his misery, but had received only evil.

30. MY SKIN . . . MY BONES: Job is describing the effect of his disease (see 2:7).

31:1. MADE A COVENANT WITH MY EYES: Job speaks here of purity toward women.

33. AS ADAM: Perhaps this is best understood "as humankind."

35. MY PROSECUTOR HAD WRITTEN A BOOK: Job wishes that God, the perfect Prosecutor who knows the allegations, had written a book that would have revealed His will and wisdom and the reasons for Job's pain. This would have cleared Job of all charges by his friends.

40. THE WORDS OF JOB ARE ENDED: The various speeches and dialogues, which began in Job 3:1, are now finished. Job had the first and last word among his friends.

UNLEASHING THE TEXT

1) What did Job mean when he said that God had "taken away" his justice (see Job 27:2; 34:5?

_____

_____

_____

_____

_____

2) According to Job 28, how can human beings acquire the wisdom of God?

_____

_____

_____

_____

_____

3) According to Job 29, what did he relish about his life prior to the tragedies he endured?

_____

_____

_____

_____

_____

4) If you were listening to Job's monologue, would you have been convinced by his defense of his own integrity? Explain.

_____

_____

_____

_____

_____

EXPLORING THE MEANING

People are right to value wisdom. Job's monologues in this middle section of the book cover a variety of topics. One of them is wisdom. Specifically, Job spends most of chapter 28 comparing the search for wisdom with the search for gold and precious stones. This comparison surely felt important to him, for he desired greater wisdom to understand his situation, and he was tired of the foolish words spoken by his companions.

Job begins by painting a vivid picture of a mining operation in search of gold, silver, copper, and so on. "Man puts an end to darkness," he says, "and searches every recess for ore in the darkness and the shadow of death" (28:3). He describes how miners cut shafts into stone and descend into the depths of the earth in search of precious metals.

Switching gears, Job then asks, "But where can wisdom be found? And where is the place of understanding?" (verse 12). Critical questions! The ultimate answer, of course, is in God. Job makes this very conclusion: "God understands its way, and He knows its place. . . . Behold, the fear of the Lord, that is wisdom, and to depart from evil is understanding" (verses 23, 28).

Job's point in these proclamations is that wisdom is extremely valuable and worthy of a diligent search—even more so than humanity's constant search for precious metals and stones. The good news for God's people is that we don't have to wear ourselves out in the search for wisdom. In fact, according to Scripture, all we need to do is ask: "If any of you lacks wisdom, let him ask of God, who gives to all liberally and without reproach, and it will be given to him" (James 1:5).

People are wrong to believe God has abandoned them. Another larger theme in Job's monologues was his belief—or at least his feeling—that God had abandoned him. "Oh, that I were as in months past," Job says, "as in the days when God watched over me; when His lamp shone upon my head, and when by His light I walked through darkness" (29:2–3). He talks about the days of his prime as, "when the Almighty was yet with me" (verse 5).

Job lists many of the ways his life had been sweeter and more meaningful before all of his personal tragedies struck. He had been respected by other men in those days, including the leaders of his city. He had served the poor and rescued the fatherless. People sought his counsel and advice, and he had given it away freely. As a result, Job had expected a long and prosperous life, filled with continued blessing and purpose. In contrast, because of his suffering, the men of Job's city now mocked him instead of respecting him. He was taunted by youths and even by feckless wanderers. He had become a shell of his former self, and he felt abandoned by God. "I cry out to You," he said, "but You do not answer me" (30:20).

One of the key principles for interpreting the Bible is never to make conclusions based on a single passage of Scripture. Instead, we allow the entire Bible to guide us. In this instance, Job genuinely felt as if God were no longer with him. In reality, we know that God was always watching over Job. (In fact, He will come to speak with Job in just a few chapters). The broader scope of Scripture makes it clear that God never abandons His people. There are dozens of passages that make it clear that "He will not leave you nor forsake you" (Deuteronomy 31:6).

People are right to value righteousness. Continuing his declarations about his past life, Job notes all the standards he had set in place to live in a way that was honoring to God. For example, he made a covenant with his eyes to avoid looking lustfully at women (see 31:1). He was constantly aware that God saw his ways and counted his steps (see verse 4).

Rhetorically, Job's language is striking. He uses a collection of if/then statements to emphasize the high priority he places on righteousness, calling down curses or punishments on himself if he had violated any of the principles he listed—often in language that is shocking. For example, "If my heart has been enticed by a woman, or if I have lurked at my neighbor's door, then let my wife grind for another, and let others bow down over her" (verses 9–10). Or, "If I have raised my hand against the fatherless, when I saw I had help in the gate; then let my arm fall from my shoulder, let my arm be torn from the socket" (verses 21–22).

Job was right to place such a high value on righteous living. In doing so, his words (and actions) mirror some of the most famous passages of the New Testament. In Romans 12:14, for example, Paul lays down the difficult standard: "Bless those who persecute you; bless and do not curse." Thousands of years prior, Job had held himself to the same standard, stating, "If I have rejoiced at the destruction of him who hated me, or lifted myself up when evil found him" (Job 31:29), he would have been guilty of "an inquity deserving of judgment" (verse 28).

REFLECTING ON THE TEXT

5) Where do you go when you need wisdom or wise counsel?

6) When have you felt as if God had abandoned you? How did God then make His presence known to you?

7) What are the primary standards you use to determine what is right and wrong?

8) How have your standards of right and wrong changed or shifted over the years?

_____

_____

_____

_____

PERSONAL RESPONSE

9) What steps can you take to ask God for wisdom this week?

_____

_____

_____

_____

10) Where have you wandered away from God's standards of righteousness? How will you get back on track?

_____

_____

_____

_____

_____

9

A DISCOURSE ON GOD'S JUSTICE

Job 32:1–34:37

DRAWING NEAR

When was a time you put your foot in your mouth because you didn't think before you spoke?

_____

_____

_____

_____

_____

_____

_____

_____

_____

THE CONTEXT

Job's story began with a brief picture of his integrity and abundant life. This was followed by accusations from Satan, and then God's allowance for Satan to destroy Job's family, work, wealth, and health. When Job's companions came to comfort him in his time of sorrow, what followed was a three-round debate in which those companions declared that Job must be guilty of great sin and should repent. Yet Job maintained his innocence and cried out to God.

Now a new participant, Elihu, comes on to the scene to enter the debate over Job's condition. Elihu is evidently a younger man who has been standing close by, watching the proceedings and listening intently as the older men strove to make their case to Job. As he opens his mouth to speak for an abundance of words, it is clear that he is frustrated and angry at the older men's failure to convince Job of their arguments. He takes a wordier (and what he considers a more "eloquent") approach to the matter and the issue of Job's suffering.

As we will discover, Elihu continues to push the older men's idea that Job had affronted God, was still affronting Him through his denials, and therefore deserved to be punished.

Keys to the Text

Read Job 32:1–34:37, noting the key words and phrases indicated below.

> *Elihu's First speech: Elihu lays the groundwork for his right to speak, his desire to do so, and promises to be forthright and impartial.*

32:1 So these three men ceased answering Job: The attempts of Job's three friends—Eliphaz, Bildad, and Zophar—to convince him of his sinfulness have failed. Job can have no more to say, having challenged God to prove his innocence. Job's three friends can also have no more to say, because they clearly consider Job a reprobate sinner and hypocrite.

2. the Buzite: Elihu's ancestry was traced to the Arabian tribe of Buz (see Jeremiah 25:23). The "family of Ram" is unknown.

4. Elihu had waited to speak: Elihu is a younger man than Job's three friends. He has been present throughout the discussions, but out of deference to his elders, he has been waiting patiently for the opportunity to speak. It is not clear, based on the text, as to why Elihu is there in the first place. The opening chapters of Job set Job in an open public space, where people can see him even from afar. It is likely that Elihu is among the bystanders who have collected nearby to listen to Job debate with his three counselors.

5. his wrath was aroused: Four times in the space of just a few verses we are told that Elihu had become angry. He is angry at Job for justifying himself (see verse 2) and at the three counselors for their inability to refute Job's arguments (see verse 3). In spite of his anger, his tone is actually less abrasive in nature as compared with many of the other speeches.

6. I WAS AFRAID, AND DARED NOT DECLARE MY OPINION: Elihu may have called his words "opinion," but he claimed they had come by inspiration from God.

8. THE BREATH OF THE ALMIGHTY GIVES HIM UNDERSTANDING: Elihu evidently believed that God had blessed him with such wisdom and understanding.

9. GREAT MEN ARE NOT ALWAYS WISE: Elihu's opening words reveal the three older counselors' reasoning had not impressed him. He pictures them as groping for words, unwise in their attempts at rebuttal, and unable to handle the debate with Job.

13. LEST YOU SAY, "WE HAVE FOUND WISDOM"; GOD WILL VANQUISH HIM, NOT MAN: Elihu appears to be accusing the counselors of saying that "God will deal with Job's wicked ways" as a way of getting out of their responsibility to debate him. However, they never made such statements.

14. I WILL NOT ANSWER HIM WITH YOUR WORDS: Elihu claims that he would have used different arguments to refute Job's statements.

18–19. FOR I AM FULL OF WORDS: Elihu's statement is true—he is "ready to burst" like a new wineskin with words—though the content of his words can be called into question. Some have noted that it takes Elihu several verses just to say, "Look, I am about to speak."

21–22: LET ME NOT . . . SHOW PARTIALITY TO ANYONE: Elihu promises that he will be absolutely impartial. In fact, he claims to not even *know* how to flatter! This young man obviously intends to be eloquent—a trait that was valued in the ancient world. Even Moses recognized the value of this kind of eloquence in speech when he complained, "O my Lord, I am not eloquent, neither before nor since You have spoken to Your servant" (Exodus 4:10). Moses pressed the issue so firmly that God eventually allowed his brother, Aaron, to speak in his place.

ELIHU'S SECOND SPEECH: Elihu now charges Job with presumption in criticizing God.

33:3. MY LIPS UTTER PURE KNOWLEDGE: Elihu continues his dissertation on the value and wisdom of his words—though again, he has said little in the way of arguments.

6. I ALSO HAVE BEEN FORMED OUT OF CLAY: Elihu here may have in mind Job's earlier words to God: "Withdraw Your hand far from me, and let not the dread of You make me afraid" (13:21). Elihu is stating that he, like Job, is a mere man formed from clay. Yet the tone of his words imply that he has taken on an attitude of superiority to Job and his three friends.

8. "SURELY YOU HAVE SPOKEN IN MY HEARING": Elihu, at long last, launches into the first of his arguments by making direct references to Job's questions and complaints.

9. "I AM INNOCENT": Job had claimed to be "blameless" (see 9:21) as it related to the great trials he was facing. He had even asked God to make known his transgressions and sins (see 13:23). But Job had never claimed to be *without* any sin.

13. HE DOES NOT GIVE AN ACCOUNTING: Job had complained that God did not speak to him. Elihu reminds Job that God does not have to defend His will or actions to anyone.

14. MAN DOES NOT PERCEIVE IT: Elihu contends that God does speak in many ways, such as through dreams and visions, to protect people from evil and deadly ways.

18. THE PIT: A reference to the realm of the dead.

19. MAN IS ALSO CHASTENED WITH PAIN: Elihu argues this is the second manner in which God speaks to people. The implication is that God has used Job's suffering as a sort of "messenger" to speak to his conscience about his sin. He avoids making the arguments of the other counselors that Job's sufferings serve as proof of his wicked ways.

23. IF THERE IS A MESSENGER FOR HIM: Job has lamented that his suffering was not deserved. Elihu answers that complaint by saying he was God's messenger. He serves as a mediator to show Job that God doesn't act in a whimsical way but allows suffering as chastening to bring a person to submit to Him, and to repent, so that the person's life may be spared.

28. HE WILL REDEEM HIS SOUL: In other words, God allows suffering for spiritual benefit.

32. I DESIRE TO JUSTIFY YOU: Elihu sided with Job and wanted to see him vindicated in his claims to righteousness, so he gave opportunity for Job to dialogue with him as he spoke.

ELIHU'S THIRD SPEECH: Elihu next declares that Job has impugned God's integrity through his claims that it does not pay to lead a godly life.

34:2. HEAR MY WORDS, YOU WISE MEN: Elihu continues to address his statements at Job and his accusers.

5. For Job has said, "I am righteous:" Elihu's approach is to quote Job directly, and then respond to his complaints. But at times, he misinterprets Job's remarks; and at other times, he puts the words of the accusers in Job's mouth.

6. "I am without transgression": The most obvious example of Elihu misinterpreting Job's words occurs here, where he states that Job claimed to be sinlessly perfect. As we have seen, Job never claimed to be sinless—in fact, he acknowledged his sin (see 7:21; 13:26). Elihu didn't know it, but God had pronounced Job innocent (see 1:8; 2:3).

9. FOR HE HAS SAID: Elihu is also incorrect in making this claim. He is putting words into Job's mouth that Job has not uttered.

10. FAR BE IT FROM GOD TO DO WICKEDNESS: In response to Job's complaints that God seems unjust, Elihu reminds him that God is too holy to do anything wrong. He is always fair (see verses 11–12), powerful (see verses 13–14), just (see verses 17–18), impartial (see verses 19–20), and omniscient (see verses 21–22).

23. GO BEFORE GOD IN JUDGMENT: These words do not refer to the judgment of the last days, but to the general accountability toward God that man experiences on a daily basis. The point Elihu is making is that God does not need to go through all the trappings of the court to get to the sentence. God already knows all the works of people (see 34:25).

31. HAS ANYONE SAID TO GOD: God will not be regulated in His dealings by what people think. He does not consult with men. If He chooses to chasten, He will decide when it is enough.

37. HE ADDS REBELLION TO HIS SIN: Apparently, Elihu is convinced that Job needs more chastening because of how he answered his prosecutors. Job continued to defend his innocence when confronted with their arguments and to appeal his innocence to God.

UNLEASHING THE TEXT

1) What are your impressions of Elihu based on these early speeches? What was he like?

_____

_____

_____

2) How are Elihu's arguments similar to those of Eliphaz, Bildad, and Zophar? How are they different?

_____

_____

_____

3) Is it wrong to complain about God or express frustration with Him? Explain.

_____

_____

_____

4) What are some statements Elihu made about God with which you agree?

_____

_____

_____

EXPLORING THE MEANING

Even the young have a right to speak. One of the noteworthy aspects of Elihu as a person was his youth. The narrator of Job's story emphasizes Elihu's youth when introducing this new character: "Now because they were years older than he, Elihu had waited to speak to Job" (32:4). Elihu himself made note of his young age: "I am young in years, and you are very old; therefore I was afraid, and dared not declare my opinion to you. I said, 'Age should speak, and multitude of years should teach wisdom'" (verses 6–7).

Still, in spite of his relative inexperience, Elihu is determined to have his say in the matter of Job's suffering. "But there is a spirit in man," he says, "and the breath of the Almighty gives him understanding. Great men are not always wise, nor do the aged always understand justice" (verses 8–9). For all his faults, Elihu is correct in these statements. God's Word makes it clear that older generations should be respected by the young. Solomon declared, "The silver-haired head is a crown of glory, If it is found in the way of righteousness" (Proverbs 16:31). Peter taught, "Likewise you younger people, submit yourselves to your elders" (1 Peter 5:5).

Yet God's Word also instructs young people to take an active role in the church and in their communities. For example, in the New Testament, Timothy was a young pastor and one of Paul's proteges. Paul said to him, "Let no one despise your youth, but be an example to the believers in word, in conduct, in love, in spirit, in faith, in purity" (1 Timothy 4:12).

Anger rarely helps solve a conflict. Another noteworthy aspect of Elihu's inclusion in this story is his anger. Right from the beginning, the text says, "Then the wrath of Elihu . . . was aroused against Job; his wrath was aroused because he justified himself rather than God. Also against his three friends his wrath was aroused, because they had found no answer, and yet had condemned Job" (32:2–3). In other words, Elihu was angry at both Job *and* his three companions, Eliphaz, Bildad, and Zophar. He was angry at Job's continued appeal to his own integrity and angry at the other three men for failing to prove Job wrong.

Elihu's speeches are born out of anger and serve as a vent for his anger—specifically at Job. "What man is like Job," he says, "Who drinks scorn like water, who goes in company with the workers of iniquity, and walks with wicked men?" (34:7–8). Later, he adds, "Oh, that Job were tried to the utmost, because his answers are like those of wicked men!" (verse 36).

In the end, Elihu's anger accomplishes little. He vents his wrath against all who will listen, and then is heard from no more. He would have been better served to abide by the principle established by King Solomon: "A soft answer turns away wrath, but a harsh word stirs up anger" (Proverbs 15:1). Or by Paul, who wrote, "Let all bitterness, wrath, anger, clamor, and evil speaking be put away from you, with all malice" (Ephesians 4:31).

In times of tragedy, silence is often more helpful than speech. It's unfortunate that Elihu did not have access to these words from the apostle James on the subject of anger and speech: "So then, my beloved brethren, let every man be swift to hear, slow to speak, slow to wrath; for the wrath of man does not produce the righteousness of God" (James 1:19–20).

As we have seen, Elihu failed at being "slow to wrath," but he was also negligent when it came to being quick to listen and slow to speak. "I am full of words," he admitted (32:18). In truth, his speeches balloon out over six chapters in Job, which is by far the longest unbroken stretch of talking from anyone in the story—including God. Even worse, Elihu didn't speak out of a desire to help Job during his time of tragedy, but simply because he could not keep his mouth shut. "Indeed my belly is like wine that has no vent. It is ready to burst like new wineskins. I will speak, that I may find relief; I must open my lips and answer" (verses 19–20).

Eliphaz, Bildad, and Zophar had been right in their desire to comfort Job. They had certainly helped when they spent seven days with him, during which "no one spoke a word to him, for they saw that his grief was very great" (2:13). Unfortunately, like Elihu, once they opened their mouths, they made things worse rather than better because they kept pushing their opinions in spite of their ignorance of what was really taking place.

REFLECTING ON THE TEXT

5) Growing up, what were you taught about respecting your elders? What have you taught others?

_____

_____

_____

6) Do you find it easy or difficult to control your anger? Explain.

_____

_____

_____

7) Why is it so difficult to hold back from speaking when we feel angry?

_____

_____

_____

_____

8) Why do we often feel compelled to speak in clichés or platitudes when we are confronted by the suffering of others?

_____

_____

_____

_____

PERSONAL RESPONSE

9) Where do you have an opportunity to simply spend time with someone who is hurting this week?

_____

_____

_____

_____

10) What steps can you take now to help you keep a hold on your tongue when you feel angry in the future?

_____

_____

_____

_____

10

A DISCOURSE ON GOD'S GREATNESS
Job 35:1–37:24

DRAWING NEAR
How do you typically respond when someone gives you bad advice?

_____

_____

_____

_____

_____

_____

_____

THE CONTEXT
In the previous session, we met a new addition to the conversation surrounding Job's tragic suffering: Elihu. A younger man, Elihu was angry at what he perceived to be Job's unrighteousness and arrogance in setting himself in a place to judge God. Elihu was also angry at Eliphaz, Bildad, and Zophar because of their inability to correct Job and set him right.

In Elihu's first three speeches, recorded in Job 32–34, he goes to great lengths to defend his right to speak (in spite of his youth) and addresses what he perceives to be Job's criticism of God. In these chapters, Elihu concludes his outburst with three more speeches that address several of Job's other complaints during his earlier interactions with his friends. It is evident that Job has raised questions that bother Elihu—especially in regard to God's justice.

In particular, Elihu condemns what he believes is Job's self-righteous attitude. He criticizes Job for claiming that he wants to be vindicated by God in one moment, and then turning around and saying that "it profits a man nothing that he should delight in God" (34:9). Of course, as we saw in the previous lesson, Job did not actually make this remark. Elihu, just like Job's three friends, has missed the point of what Job is attempting to say.

Elihu finishes with a lengthy discussion on God's goodness, works, wisdom, and majesty. His point is to show Job that humans cannot even comprehend God's works in the natural world. So how can they hope to understand the deeper mysteries of God's providence?

KEYS TO THE TEXT

Read Job 35:1–37:24, noting the key words and phrases indicated below.

> FOURTH SPEECH: *Elihu again refers to Job's earlier complaints against God. He does not restate Job's exact words but rather summarizes his main viewpoints.*

35:2. DO YOU SAY, "MY RIGHTEOUSNESS IS MORE THAN GOD'S": This can also be translated, "You say, 'I will be cleared by God'" (as in the *New International Version*). Job has frequently expressed his belief that he will eventually be vindicated before God (see, for example, Job 13:13–19).

3. FOR YOU SAY, "WHAT ADVANTAGE WILL IT BE TO YOU?": Job had also previously indicated that there appears to be no advantage in being righteous (see, for example, 21:15; 34:9). Although Job never asked, "What profit shall I have, more than if I had sinned," Elihu is deriving it from Job's complaint that God seems to treat the wicked and the righteous alike. Elihu interprets Job's words to mean that he is accusing God of being unjust.

7 IF YOU ARE RIGHTEOUS, WHAT DO YOU GIVE HIM: Elihu argues that Job gains nothing by sinning or not sinning, because God is so high above humans that nothing anyone does can affect him. Neither sins of commission nor omission have any impact on the Almighty God.

8. YOUR WICKEDNESS AFFECTS A MAN SUCH AS YOU: The sins of people thus only affect other people. Elihu leaves no place for a person to do God's will

out of love for Him, nor does he consider God as a loving father who can be hurt or pleased by a person's actions. Elihu only views God in the role of a judge who enforces the rules and maintains justice.

9. BECAUSE OF THE MULTITUDE OF OPPRESSIONS THEY CRY OUT: Job had complained that God did not answer his prayers when he cried out under his oppression (see 24:12; 30:20). Elihu restates Job's sentiment here before providing his view on why this might be happening.

10. SONGS IN THE NIGHT: Most likely songs of praise as a result of deliverance. "The LORD will command His lovingkindness in the daytime, and in the night His song shall be with me—a prayer to the God of my life" (Psalm 42:8).

12. BECAUSE OF THE PRIDE OF EVIL MEN: Elihu now provides three reasons why, in his opinion, Job's prayers have not been heard. The first reason is due to his *pride*.

13. GOD WILL NOT LISTEN TO EMPTY TALK: The second reason why Job's prayers have not been answered is due to his *wrong motives*. Elihu holds that God does not listen to the cries of people when they come to him as "empty talk."

14. YOU MUST WAIT FOR HIM: The third reason why Job's prayers have not been answered is due to a lack of *patient trust*. Elihu appears to be offended by the idea that Job would consider himself as a litigant in God's court and views it as a sign of Job's pride. Given this attitude, Job should not expect to be heard by the Almighty. Again, all of Elihu's theoretical talk misses Job's predicament, because Job is righteous. Elihu is no more help than the other counselors.

15 HE HAS NOT PUNISHED IN HIS ANGER: Elihu suggests that although Job has suffered, his suffering is not the fullness of God's anger, or else He would have been additionally punished for the sinfulness of his speeches. Elihu actually argues here that God has not "taken much notice" of Job's folly in his useless words.

> FIFTH SPEECH: *Elihu now turns from condemning Job to providing his opinions on God's goodness, mercy, and majesty.*

36:2. THERE ARE YET WORDS TO SPEAK ON GOD'S BEHALF: Elihu had agreed with his three co-counselors that Job was guilty of sinning, if nowhere else than (1) in the way Job questioned God (see 33:12), (2) by seeing his suffering as indicative that God is unjust (see 34:34–37), and (3) by feeling that righteousness has no reward (see 35:2–16). In this final answer to Job, he now turns to focus mostly on God rather than the sufferer. He is somewhat apologetic over the fact that he has even more to say in defense of God—asking Job to "bear with" him—though he had previously claimed to be "full of words" (32:18).

4. ONE WHO IS PERFECT IN KNOWLEDGE: Elihu makes what appears to be an outrageous claim about himself in order to give credibility to his remarks.

6. BUT GIVES JUSTICE: Elihu begins by repeating the thought that though God sends trouble at times, He is always just and merciful.

7. HE DOES NOT WITHDRAW HIS EYES FROM THE RIGHTEOUS: Elihu appears to be making some room for Job's complaints about the suffering of the righteous. God never takes his eyes off the righteous. However, he may discipline them at times for their own good.

9. HE TELLS THEM . . . THEIR TRANSGRESSIONS: God convicts the righteous of their sins.

10. HE ALSO OPENS THEIR EAR TO INSTRUCTION: The Hebrew word for *instruction* refers to the actions that God takes to teach His wisdom to humans. "For the commandment is a lamp, and the law a light; reproofs of instruction are the way of life" (Proverbs 6:23). God may use "cords of affliction" (verse 8) or other means of correction to compel people to turn from their sins.

11–12. IF THEY OBEY . . . BUT IF THEY DO NOT OBEY: God rewards people's obedience but punishes their rebellion. Obedience leads to life, while disobedience leads to death.

15. OPENS THEIR EARS IN OPPRESSION: This is a new insight from Elihu and perhaps the most helpful thing that he has said to Job. Elihu goes beyond all that has been previously spoken about God using suffering to chasten and bring repentance. He is saying that God uses suffering to open people's ears and draw them to Himself.

16. HE WOULD HAVE BROUGHT YOU OUT OF DIRE DISTRESS: However, Elihu holds that as long as Job keeps complaining, he is turning to iniquity rather than drawing nearer to God in his suffering. So, while Elihu disagrees with the claim that the wicked prosper, he agrees with Job that the righteous do at times suffer—though this is caused by their sins, which must be corrected. Elihu thus

holds out hope that Job can be delivered if he recognizes God is using his suffering to compel him to repent of sin and turn back to him.

17. YOU ARE FILLED WITH THE JUDGMENT DUE THE WICKED: Elihu does not want Job to allow his suffering to influence his judgment.

> *SIXTH SPEECH: Elihu makes his final appeal in response to Job's suffering and his claims of righteousness.*

22. WHO TEACHES LIKE HIM: Elihu remarks that Job, instead of complaining and questioning God, which was sin (as Job will later confess), he needed to see God in his suffering and worship Him. Job needed to learn the lesson that God was teaching him through affliction.

26. WE DO NOT KNOW HIM: Although people may have personal knowledge of God in salvation, the fullness of His glory is beyond human comprehension.

27. HE DRAWS UP DROPS OF WATER: Elihu gives a picture of God's power in the rainstorm.

31. JUDGES ... GIVES FOOD: The rainstorm can be a disaster of punishment from God or a source of abundant crops.

37.5–6: GOD THUNDERS ... HE SAYS TO THE SNOW: Elihu describes God's power in the thunderstorm and the cold winter. These events remind people of the world in which harsh things occur, but that can happen for God's good purposes of either *correction* or *mercy*.

17. WHEN HE QUIETS THE EARTH: Elihu describes the scene in the sky when the storms have passed, the sunlight breaks through, the warm wind blows, and the sky clears.

19. TEACH US WHAT WE SHOULD SAY TO HIM: Elihu reminds Job that because humans can't explain the wonders of God's power, they should be silent and not contend with Him. What a person has to say against God's plans is not worthy to utter and could bring judgment.

21. CANNOT LOOK AT THE LIGHT: Elihu illustrates the folly of humans attempting to tell God what to do by describing staring into the golden sun on a brilliant day. Humans cannot confront God in His great glory. They are not even able to look directly at the sun He created.

24. SHOWS NO PARTIALITY: God is the righteous Judge who will not take a bribe or perform favors in judgment. Thus, in this concluding speech, Elihu points Job and the reader to God, who was ready, at last, to speak.

UNLEASHING THE TEXT

1) What point was Elihu trying to make through his rhetorical questions in Job 35?

_____

_____

_____

_____

2) In what ways did Elihu try to defend God against what he believed to be Job's attacks?

_____

_____

_____

_____

3) How did Elihu's imagery in Job 36 and 37 communicate God's goodness and majesty?

_____

_____

_____

_____

4) Where do you find yourself agreeing with Elihu? Why?

_____

_____

_____

_____

EXPLORING THE MEANING

We cannot harm God with our sin. Elihu, continuing in the footsteps of Job and his companions, spent a lot of time in his speeches to declare his opinions about God's nature and character. One interesting example occurs when he asks,

"If you sin, what do you accomplish against Him? Or, if your transgressions are multiplied, what do you do to Him?" (35:6).

Elihu's question is interesting for two reasons. First, he is correct in the principle he wishes to communicate—namely, that God is not harmed or affected by human sin. The Bible reveals that God is grieved when humans sin out of His love for us (see Genesis 6:6; Psalm 95:10; Isaiah 63:10). But we cannot elevate ourselves above God in our own minds by thinking our mistakes and failures impact Him in some way. In reality, God is far above all created things. "[He] is the same yesterday, today, and forever" (Hebrews 13:8).

A second reason why Elihu's argument is interesting is because he ignores his own advice and attacks Job on God's behalf. Elihu believes that Job has affronted God, so he appoints himself as God's defender. "Bear with me a little," he says, "and I will show you that *there are* yet words to speak on God's behalf" (36:2). In the process, he forgets his own argument about God's majesty and power!

God does not need human defenders, because He cannot be harmed by created things. If God decides we need to be corrected or disciplined, He will step in to make it happen in the way that He knows to be best. This is a truth that He would yet demonstrate to both Job and Elihu in the final act of the story.

We cannot help God with our righteousness. Not only did Elihu make the case that human transgressions can have no impact on God, but he also rightly pointed out the same is true for human goodness. "If you are righteous, what do you give Him? Or what does He receive from your hand?" (35:7). Ultimately, we come to recognize that God is above us in every way.

Once again, it is easy for us to elevate our own importance in our minds by believing that God will somehow be improved or blessed by our obedience. But the reality is that God does not need anything from us. Therefore, there is nothing we provide to Him when we choose to obey His will. Jesus reminded His followers of this truth when He compared people to servants who expect to be rewarded for doing their job. "So likewise you, when you have done all those things which you are commanded, say, 'We are unprofitable servants. We have done what was our duty to do'" (Luke 17:10).

All of this is not to say that God is distant from humanity, or that He doesn't care about our actions. Quite the contrary. Both Old and New Testaments repeatedly stress God's tender, compassionate love for us. "The LORD is good to all, and His tender mercies are over all His works" (Psalm 145:9). "God demonstrates His own love toward us, in that while we were still sinners, Christ died for us" (Romans 5:8).

The fact that God sent His beloved Son to die to pay the atonement price for sin is the ultimate proof that God is not distant or indifferent to humanity. The best-known verse of the New Testament makes that very point: "God so loved the world that He gave His only begotten Son, that whoever believes in Him should not perish but have everlasting life. For God did not send His Son into the world to condemn the world, but that the world through Him might be saved" (John 3:16-17).

God sometimes uses suffering to catch our attention. What was the reason for Job's suffering? What was the source? This question serves as the foundation for the entire argument between Job and the four men (including Elihu) who evaluated his life. Eliphaz, Bildad, and Zophar had been adamant in their belief that the magnitude of Job's suffering meant he was being punished. In their minds, suffering was *always* a punishment for sin.

Elihu introduces a different idea when he states that God "delivers the poor in their affliction, and opens their ears in oppression" (36:15). This is a new idea in the context of Job's story. Elihu had earlier noted that God actively steers people away from sin by opening their ears to "instruction" and commanding them to avoid iniquity (see verse 10). He went on to expand on this idea by claiming that God sometimes uses adverse situations—poverty and oppression, in this example—as a way to draw people to Himself (see verse 15).

Elihu was right in identifying this general principle. God does use suffering as one of the tools to catch our attention and drawa us close to Him. Paul highlighted this principle when he taught early church leaders how to deal with Christians who were willfully living in rebellion against God: "Deliver such a one to Satan for the destruction of the flesh, that his spirit may be saved in the day of the Lord Jesus" (1 Corinthians 5:5). Paul wanted Christians who openly sinned to experience the consequences of their sin so they would return to God.

Just like Job's other three companions, Elihu was correct in identifying a general principle but incorrect in applying that principle to Job's life. Yes, God sometimes uses suffering to guide us toward Himself. In Job's case, however, the suffering he experienced was a direct attack by Satan—not a result of Job's wrongdoing.

REFLECTING ON THE TEXT

5) Why is it important to understand that we can't impact God by our righteousness or unrighteousness?

_____

_____

_____

6) What are some ways that Christians today try to stand up for God or defend Him against the attacks of others?

_____

_____

_____

7) Is it helpful or unhelpful for Christians to defend God in this way? What are the consequences?

_____

_____

_____

8) When has God used suffering or loss as a way of getting your attention or drawing you into closer fellowship with Him?

_____

_____

_____

PERSONAL RESPONSE

9) Where are you currently trying to "help" God or make Him like you better through your own righteousness?

_____

_____

_____

10) How can you be alert for circumstances—even tragedy or suffering—that God uses to catch your attention or guide you in the right direction?

_____

_____

_____

_____

11

THE DELIVERANCE
Job 38:1–43:34

DRAWING NEAR
What is one of your most memorable encounters with God? What made it memorable?

_____

_____

_____

_____

_____

_____

THE CONTEXT
The majority of Job's story reveals the futility of human wisdom and thinking. For chapter after chapter, five men spoke at one another, made accusations, and offered rebuttals. For hundreds of verses, Job, Eliphaz, Bildad, Zophar, and eventually Elihu all spun their wheels and failed to make progress on the central question of the book: *Why do righteous people suffer?*

The situation suddenly changes in Job 38, because God shows up on the scene. In many ways, Job's entire story has been building to this moment: a confrontation with God as Judge. Job finally gets the day in court he has been asking for—the chance to plead his case and the chance to hear God answer his questions and complaints.

God offers four responses in the final chapters of Job. First, he asks a series of questions designed to reveal the difference between Job and Himself. Second,

He uses two mighty creatures, Behemoth and Leviathan, to illustrate His own power. Third, He confronts Job's four companions, declaring them to be wrong in their assertions about Job's character. Finally, He restores Job's health, wealth, and family to levels beyond what he had known previously.

KEYS TO THE TEXT

Read Job 38:1–43:34, noting the key words and phrases indicated below.

> GOD'S FIRST RESPONSE: *God begins his interrogation of Job by asking many pointed questions.*

38:1. OUT OF THE WHIRLWIND: Job had repeatedly called God to court in order to verify his innocence. God finally arrives to interrogate Job on some of the comments he had made. God was about to be Job's vindicator, but He first brought Job to a right understanding of Himself.

2. WHO DARKENS COUNSEL: Job's words had only further confused matters that were already muddled by useless counselors.

3. I WILL QUESTION YOU: God silences Job's presumption in constantly wanting to ask Him questions by becoming Job's questioner. It is important to note that God never tells Job about the reason for his pain (the conflict between Himself and Satan). He simply asks Job if he is as eternal, great, powerful, wise, and perfect as Him. If not, it would have been better if Job had simply kept quiet and trusted in Him.

4. THE FOUNDATIONS OF THE EARTH: God asks Job if he participated in creation, as He did. This is a humbling query with an obvious *no* answer.

5. DETERMINED ITS MEASUREMENTS: Creation is spoken of using the language of building construction.

7. MORNING STARS . . . SONS OF GOD: The angelic realm, God's ministering spirits.

8. WHO SHUT IN THE SEA: God describes His power over the sea by raising the continents, along with the thick clouds that draw up its water to carry rain to the land.

12. COMMANDED THE MORNING: The dawn rises, and as it spreads light over the earth, it exposes the wicked, much like shaking the corners of a cloth exposes dirt.

14. CLAY UNDER A SEAL: Documents written on clay tablets were signed using engraved seals on which was written the bearer's name. The Hebrew for "takes on form" is turned. It conveys the idea that the earth is turned or rotated like a cylindrical seal rolled over the soft clay. Such rolling cylinder seals were found in Babylon. This speaks of the earth, rotating on its axis, an amazing statement that only God could reveal in ancient days.

15. THEIR LIGHT: The light of the wicked is darkness, because that is when they do their works. The dawn takes away their opportunity to do their deeds and stops their uplifted arm that is ready to harm. Was Job around when God created this light?

22. TREASURY: The storehouse of these elements is the clouds.

31–32. PLEIADES . . . ORION . . . MAZZAROTH . . . GREAT BEAR: Stellar constellations.

33. ORDINANCES OF THE HEAVENS: The laws and powers that regulate all heavenly bodies.

36. WISDOM . . . UNDERSTANDING: This is the heart of the issue. The wisdom of God, which created and sustains the universe, is also at work in Job's suffering.

39. CAN YOU HUNT THE PREY: God now asks Job humiliating questions about whether he could take care of the animal kingdom. Job must have been feeling less and less significant under the crushing indictment of such comparisons with God.

39:5. ONAGER: A wild donkey.

13. THE OSTRICH: This silly bird that leaves her eggs on the ground lacks sense. God has not given her wisdom. She is almost a picture of Job, who is a mixture of foolishness and strength.

19. THE HORSE: A vivid picture of a war horse is in view here.

40:2. LET HIM ANSWER IT: God challenges Job to answer all the questions he has posed. God already knew the answer, but Job needed to admit his weakness, inferiority, and inability to try to figure out God's infinite mind. God's wisdom was so superior, His sovereign control of everything so complete, that this was all Job needed to know.

3. THEN JOB ANSWERED: Job's first response to God is, "I am guilty as charged. I will say no more." He knows he should not have found fault with the Almighty. He should not have insisted on his own understanding. He should not have thought God unjust.

GOD'S SECOND RESPONSE: God continues to query Job, this time with a focus on two specific animals that represent God's power.

8. WOULD YOU INDEED: God unleashes another torrent of crushing rebukes to Job. He mocks Job's questionings of Him, telling Him that if he *really* thought he knew what was best for him rather than God, then he should take over being God!

15. THE BEHEMOTH: While this is a generic term used commonly in the Old Testament for large cattle or land animals, the description in this passage suggests an extraordinary creature. The hippopotamus has been suggested by the details in the passage (see verses 19–24). However, the short tail of a hippo is hardly consistent with verse 17, where *tail* could be translated "trunk." It might refer to an elephant, who could easily be considered "first" or chief of God's creatures whom only He can control. Some believe God is describing His most impressive creation among land animals, the dinosaur species, which fit all the characteristics.

23. THE RIVER MAY RAGE: God was not saying this creature lived in the Jordan River, but rather used it to illustrate how much water this beast could ingest. He could swallow the Jordan! It was a word used to refer to something of enormous size and threatening power.

41:1. LEVIATHAN: This term appears four other places in the Old Testament (Job 3:8; Psalm 74:14; 104:26; Isaiah 27:1). In each case, it refers to a mighty creature that can overwhelm humans but is no match for God. This creature lived in the sea among ships (see Psalm 104:26), so some form of sea monster, and possibly an ancient dinosaur, is in view. Some have held it was a crocodile, which has a scaly hide and terrible teeth (see 41:14–15), but crocodiles are not deep-sea creatures, and clearly this one was (see verse 31). Others have thought it was a killer whale or a great white shark, which are the ultimate killer beasts over all other proud beasts (see verse 34).

4. WILL HE MAKE A COVENANT WITH YOU: God was asking, "Will this monstrous creature need, for any reason, to come to terms with you, Job? Are you able to control him?"

10. WHO THEN IS ABLE TO STAND AGAINST ME? This was the essential question being asked in both the Behemoth and Leviathan passages. God created these awesome creatures, and His might is far greater than theirs. If Job couldn't stand against them, what was he doing contending with God? He would be better off to fight a dinosaur or a killer shark.

11. THAT I SHOULD PAY HIM: God does not need to buy anything, for He already owns all things. Paul quoted this in his letter to the Romans: "Who has first given to Him and it shall be repaid to him" (Romans 11:35).

REBUKE ACCEPTED: Job accepts God's correction and passes judgment on himself.

42:2. I KNOW THAT YOU CAN DO EVERYTHING: Job's confession and repentance finally take place. He still does not know why he suffered so profoundly, but he quits complaining, questioning, and challenging God's wisdom and justice. He is reduced to such utter humility, crushed beneath the weight of God's greatness, that all he could do was repent for his insolence. Without answers to all of his questions, he bowed in humble submission before his Creator and admitted that God was sovereign.

3-4. YOU ASKED . . . YOU SAID: Job twice alludes to statements God had in His interrogation of him. The first allusion, "Who is this who hides counsel without knowledge" (38:2), indicted Job's pride and presumption about God's counsel. The second, "I will question you, and you shall answer Me" (38:3; 40:7), expressed God's judicial authority to demand answers from His own accuser, Job. The two quotes show that Job understood the divine rebuke.

5. HAVE HEARD . . . NOW MY EYE SEES YOU: At last, Job says he understands God, whom he has seen with the eyes of faith. He had never grasped the greatness, majesty, sovereignty, and independence of God as well as he did in this moment.

6. REPENT IN DUST AND ASHES: All that is left to do was repent! Job did not need to repent of some sins that Satan or his accusers had raised. But he had exercised presumption and allegations of unfairness against his Lord, and hated himself for this in a way that called for brokenness and contrition.

FINAL WORDS AND RESTORATION: God rebukes all four of Job's companions and then restores the abundance of Job's life to new heights.

7. YOU HAVE NOT SPOKEN OF ME WHAT IS RIGHT: God vindicates Job, saying he has spoken correctly about Him. God then rebukes Job's friends for their misrepresentations and arrogance. This does not mean everything they said

was incorrect, but they had made wrong statements about God's character and works and had raised erroneous allegations against Job.

8. SEVEN BULLS AND SEVEN RAMS: Since this was the number of sacrifices specified in Numbers 23:1 by Balaam the prophet, it was perhaps a traditional kind of burnt offering for sin.

9. WENT AND DID AS THE LORD COMMANDED: As God had been gracious to Job, so He was gracious to Job's friends, by means of sacrifice and prayer. Here, the book points to the need for a sacrifice for sin, fulfilled in the Lord Jesus Christ who gave Himself as an offering for sins and ever lives to intercede (see 1 Timothy 2:5). Even before the Levitical priesthood, family heads acted as priests, offering sacrifices and mediating through prayer.

13. SEVEN SONS . . . THREE DAUGHTERS: The animals are double the number of Job 1:3, but not the children. Job still has seven sons and three daughters waiting for him in the presence of God (see verse 17).

14. JEMIMAH . . . KEZIAH . . . KEREN-HAPPUCH: These names are representative of the joys of restoration. *Jemimah* means "day light," *Keziah* means "sweet smelling," and *Keren-Happuch* describes a beautiful color that women used to paint their eyelids.

15. GAVE THEM AN INHERITANCE: This was unusual in the East. By Jewish law, daughters received an inheritance only when there were no sons. Job had plenty for all.

17. SO JOB DIED, OLD AND FULL OF DAYS: These concluding words take the reader back to where the account began (see 1:1). Job died in prosperity, and his days were counted as a blessing. He experienced the outcome of the Lord's dealings, that the Lord is "very compassionate and merciful" (James 5:11). But the "accuser of our brethren" (Revelation 12:10) is still "going to and fro on the earth" (Job 1:7), and God's servants are still learning to trust in the all-wise, all-powerful Judge of the universe for what they cannot understand.

UNLEASHING THE TEXT

1) What are your first impressions of God based on Job 38?

_____

_____

_____

_____

2) What are some of the key points that God raised during His response to Job?

_____

_____

_____

_____

3) How should we understand God's references to animals and the natural world throughout His speeches?

_____

_____

_____

_____

4) What stands out most about Job's response to God in Job 42? Why?

_____

_____

_____

_____

EXPLORING THE MEANING

God is all-powerful and wise. The central theme in God's response is His power and sovereignty as Creator of all things. God demonstrated that power first and foremost by speaking to Job and his companions "out of the whirlwind" (38:1). As Jesus later demonstrated, God is in complete control of the forces of nature—even tempests (see Mark 4:35–41).

God's response to Job consists primarily of rhetorical questions. "Where were you when I laid the foundations of the Earth?" He asks. "Tell Me, if you have understanding. Who determined its measurements? (Job 38:4–5). "Have the gates of death been revealed to you? Or have you seen the doors of the shadow of death?" (verse 17). "Does the hawk fly by your wisdom, and spread its wings toward the south? Does the eagle mount up at your command, and make its nest on high?" (39:26–27). God's purpose in asking these questions is to highlight His power and wisdom in relation to Job's weakness and humanity.

God speaks frequently of animals in His response. Two animals in particular represent His power. *Behemoth* is described as a land animal that "moves his tail like a cedar . . . his bones are like beams of bronze, His ribs like bars of iron" (40:17–18). *Leviathan* is a sea creature with "terrible teeth" (41:14) and "rows of scales" (verse 15) whose "breath kindles coals" and "a flame goes out of his mouth" (verse 21). God asks, "Can you put a reed through his nose, or pierce his jaw with a hook? Will he make many supplications to you? Will he speak softly to you?" (verses 2–3). The implication is that if Behemoth and Leviathan are beyond humanity's ability to contain or control, how much more the God who created them?

Taken together, God's response to Job is a definitive statement on His immeasurable strength, wisdom, and experience when it comes to running the universe.

God is personal and loving. However, God's message to Job and his companions goes beyond just His majesty and power. We also discover His personal attention and love for humanity. It is incredible to think that the Creator and Sustainer of the universe—the same being who laid the foundations of the earth and governs the lives of every kind of creature—would take the time not only to observe Job's suffering but also respond to his complaints and desire for answers. God's response to Job was in and of itself an act of love.

The text also reveals God's personal care for Job, and by extension His love for all humanity. Back in Job 1:1, we read that Job is a man who "feared God and shunned evil." The Hebrew word translated "God" in that verse is *Yahweh*, which is God's covenantal name. It is the name He gave to Moses at the burning bush: "I AM WHO I AM" (Exodus 3:14).

However, in most of Job's story, a different name is used for God: *El Shaddai*. This name means "God the Almighty." This is significant, because when Job and his companions speak of God, they are talking about a distant being—the Almighty Creator who is set apart from creation. The language shows the distance in the relationship between God and humanity.

Yet when God speaks to Job "out of the whirlwind" (38:1), He returns to the name *Yahweh*. The language of God's name shows Him coming near and acting out of His personal connection to humanity as a whole, and to Job individually. God's personal, covenantal name reveals His personal, relational connection to and care for Job. It reveals the same to us.

God Himself is the answer to the question of suffering. Why does suffering exist in the world? This is the critical question at the heart of Job's story. Yet, as we have seen, it is never answered—not even by God. Throughout Job, we are shown sources for suffering. Sometimes we experience tragedy because of Satan's attacks. Sometimes we suffer because we are being punished for our sin. Other times we suffer because God wants to catch our attention or because we are affected by the wicked choices of others.

In short, there is no universal cause for suffering. But there is a universal response to suffering. And that response is to trust in God. Job's story reveals that suffering and tragedy are real—yet they do not exist in a vacuum. We live in a universe created by a sovereign, wise, all-powerful God. We are drawn to that God because He loves us and graciously brings us into relationship with Him. Therefore, no matter what we experience in this life, we can leave the question of "why?" in His hands and simply trust that He is in control.

REFLECTING ON THE TEXT

5) What are some ways you have experienced the power and majesty of God?

_____

_____

_____

_____

6) What are some ways you have experienced God's personal love and care?

_____

_____

_____

_____

7) How would you summarize the message or moral of Job's story?

_____

_____

_____

_____

_____

8) Do you feel satisfied by the answer to the question, "why does suffering exist"? Explain.

_____

_____

_____

_____

PERSONAL RESPONSE

9) How should the reality of God's power and wisdom impact your life this week?

_____

_____

_____

_____

10) What steps do you need to take right now to deepen your fellowship with *Yahweh*, who desires to know you and be known by you?

_____

_____

_____

_____

12

REVIEWING KEY PRINCIPLES

DRAWING NEAR

As you think back over Job's story, what surprised you the most? Why?

_____

_____

_____

_____

_____

_____

_____

_____

_____

_____

THE CONTEXT

On the one hand, Job's story is both long and complex. It reveals the ups and downs of human understanding both in Job's time and today. It reveals the reality of suffering and the philosophical lengths that we as humans traverse as we seek to understand the roots of evil and righteousness in our world. It also offers glimpses into our desire as people to understand, to be heard, to be seen as we are, and to be comforted in our loss.

Yet on the other hand, Job's story is profoundly simple. After experiencing the attacks of an unknown enemy, Job just wanted to know that God was real and in control. He wanted to be assured that—somehow and in some way—everything would be okay. The same is true for us today as we navigate a world that is still suffering under the oppression and suppression of our enemy. Thankfully, Job's story shines a light on the most important truth we can understand in our present darkness: *God is real, He is control, and He loves us.* Therefore, we can trust Him.

The following represent a few of the major principles we have uncovered during our study. There are many more we don't have room to reiterate, so take some time to review the earlier studies—or, better still, to meditate on the passages of Scripture that we have covered. As you do, ask the Holy Spirit to give you wisdom and insight into His Word. He will not refuse.

EXPLORING THE MEANING

God knows His children. One truth that stands out from Job is that God is fully aware of our lives. He sees us and knows our actions, our conversations, and even our thoughts. There is nothing that escapes His attention and nothing about us He does not comprehend.

What an amazing truth! God is the Creator of everything that exists—worlds upon worlds, galaxies upon galaxies, and more. Not only that, but God sustains all that exists. Were God to remove Himself from creation at any point, everything we know would crumble and fade—just like the picture on your TV winks out as soon as you unplug the power cord.

Yet in spite of everything that requires God's attention, He still has the capacity and the interest to follow the details of a single human life such as Job. God even pointed Job out to Satan, noting that he was "a blameless and upright man, one who fears God and shuns evil" (1:8). God knew Job intimately. He knows each of us intimately as well.

Humanity needs a mediator. Job responded to Bildad's call to repent by lamenting the distance he felt between himself and God. He extolled God's majesty, power, and righteousness, and then he asked, "How then can I answer Him, and choose my words to reason with Him?" (9:14). Job longed to make his case before God as his Judge. Yet he felt as if he had no access to the Almighty—no way to approach Him and beg for mercy.

Job's description of his plight near the end of chapter 9 is especially poignant: "For He is not a man, as I am, that I may answer Him, and that we should go to court together. Nor is there any mediator between us, who may lay his hand on us both" (verses 32–33). Without realizing it, Job was pointing forward to the work of Jesus as the Messiah.

Paul would later emphasize this element of Jesus' ministry when he wrote, "For there is one God and one Mediator between God and men, the Man Christ Jesus, who gave Himself a ransom for all, to be testified in due time" (1 Timothy 2:5–6). On the cross, Jesus accepted the wages of sin—death. Thus, He paid the price of redemption for all who believe. Therefore, Scripture says, "He is also able to save to the uttermost those who come to God through Him, since He always lives to make intercession for them" (Hebrews 7:25), and, "if anyone sins, we have an Advocate with the Father, Jesus Christ the righteous" (1 John 2:1). In other words, Christ has provided exactly what Job longed to find.

It is appropriate to express our emotions to God. For most of the conversations between Job and his friends, Job addresses his responses and rebuttals to his companions. He speaks first to Eliphaz, and then to Bildad, and then to Zophar. At times, however, Job turns his attention and his words directly to God. These words are included in the second half of Job 14.

What does Job say to God in those verses? Primarily, he expresses the deep and bitter anguish of his soul. "Oh, that You would hide me in the grave," he says, speaking to God. "That You would conceal me until Your wrath is past, that You would appoint me a set time, and remember me!" (verse 13). He expresses to God his confusion and frustration with everything that has happened to him. Job feels as if God has destroyed his hope in the same way that rockslides destroy a mountain slope and water wears away stone (verses 18–19).

Job was not being melodramatic in these expressions, nor was he making accusations or casting aspersions toward God. Instead, he was openly and honestly pouring himself out to the Lord, believing and trusting that God had heard him. This is a pure form of prayer—and it is one Christians should emulate today. When we feel hopeless, frustrated, or angry about our circumstances, we don't help ourselves by pushing those feelings down and trying to act pious or "spiritual." We do better to cry out to God, just as Job did. After all, the Lord already knows what we are feeling! And He has the power to bring comfort and peace.

There is value in repentance. In his third speech, Eliphaz is particularly insulting to Job, labeling him as a man of great "wickedness" and "iniquity without end" (22:5). He accuses Job of stripping poor people of their clothes, withholding food from the hungry, refusing to help widows, and more. His goal, as before, is to push Job toward repentance.

In speaking on this subject, Eliphaz correctly and even eloquently describes the benefits of coming before God to repent of our sin. "If you return to the Almighty, you will be built up," he states. "You will remove iniquity far from your tents" (verse 23). He adds, "For then you will have your delight in the Almighty, and lift up your face to God. You will make your prayer to Him, He will hear you, and you will pay your vows" (verses 26–27).

In spite of Eliphaz's flaws as a comforter, uplifting the benefits of repentance is a thoroughly biblical principle. In fact, Jesus began His public ministry by proclaiming, "Repent, for the kingdom of heaven is at hand" (Matthew 4:17). The disciple Peter urged, "Repent therefore and be converted, that your sins may be blotted out, so that times of refreshing may come from the presence of the Lord" (Acts 3:19). The Bible is filled with the stories of people like David who honestly repented of their sin and were restored to fellowship with God.

In short, we are all guilty of sin. Therefore, when we make mistakes, we can confidently take Eliphaz's advice and come before God's throne to repent. As the author of Hebrews stated, "Let us therefore come boldly to the throne of grace, that we may obtain mercy and find grace to help in time of need" (Hebrews 4:16). God will welcome us when we take such action, and He has already made provision for our forgiveness.

Our Redeemer lives! In the midst of Job's response to Bildad and Zophar, he makes an incredible declaration of faith: "For I know that my Redeemer lives, and He shall stand at last on the earth; and after my skin is destroyed, this I know, that in my flesh I shall see God" (Job 19:25–26). These words are striking for many reasons, one of which is that Job spoke them in the midst of his intense sorrow and despair.

In Hebrew culture, a *redeemer* was someone—typically a family member—who was willing to pay a price in order to secure another's freedom. For instance, if someone had been forced to sell their home in order to pay a debt, a family member could step in and redeem that property by essentially pur-chasing it back for the original owner.

In one sense, then, Job was expressing confidence that God would even-tually step in on his behalf and "redeem" his integrity. Eliphaz, Bildad, and Zophar had continually proclaimed him to be guilty of great sin against God. But Job fully believed that God Himself would intervene to vindicate him and declare him free of any wrongdoing.

More importantly, Job's words are a powerful prophecy that point to Jesus and the gospel. By willingly offering Himself as a sacrifice on the cross, Jesus paid the price for the sin of those who will be saved, and He redeemed them through His blood. Job was correct that his Redeemer lives and would "stand at last on the earth." Those promises were ultimately fulfilled in Christ.

People are right to value righteousness. Continuing his declarations about his past life, Job notes all the standards he had set in place to live in a way that was honoring to God. For example, he made a covenant with his eyes to avoid looking lustfully at women (see 31:1). He was constantly aware that God saw his ways and counted his steps (see verse 4).

Rhetorically, Job's language is striking. He uses a collection of if/then statements to emphasize the high priority he places on righteousness, calling down curses or punishments on himself if he had violated any of the principles he listed—often in language that is shocking. For example, "If my heart has been enticed by a woman, or if I have lurked at my neighbor's door, then let my wife grind for another, and let others bow down over her" (verses 9–10). Or, "If I have raised my hand against the fatherless, when I saw I had help in the gate; then let my arm fall from my shoulder, let my arm be torn from the socket" (verses 21–22).

Job was right to place such a high value on righteous living. In doing so, his words (and actions) mirror some of the most famous passages of the New Testament. In Romans 12:14, for example, Paul lays down a standard that still feels difficult to meet today: "Bless those who persecute you; bless and do not curse." Job made the same standard for himself, stating, "If I have rejoiced at the destruction of him who hated me, or lifted myself up when evil found him" (Job 31:29), he would then accept whatever punishment God allotted for him.

Anger rarely helps solve a conflict. Another noteworthy aspect of Elihu's in-clusion in this story is his anger. Right from the beginning, the text says, "Then the wrath of Elihu . . . was aroused against Job; his wrath was aroused because he justified himself rather than God. Also against his three friends his wrath was aroused, because they had found no answer, and yet had con-demned Job" (32:2–3). In other words, Elihu was angry at both Job *and* his three companions, Eliphaz, Bildad, and Zophar. He was angry at Job's contin-ued appeal to his own integrity and angry at the other three men for failing to prove Job wrong.

Elihu's speeches are born out of anger and serve as a vent for his anger—specifically at Job. "What man is like Job," he says, "who drinks scorn like water, who goes in company with the workers of iniquity, and walks with wicked men?" (34:7–8). Later, he adds, "Oh, that Job were tried to the utmost, because his answers are like those of wicked men!" (verse 36).

In the end, Elihu's anger accomplishes little. He vents his wrath against all who will listen, and then is heard from no more. He would have been better served to abide by the principle established by King Solomon: "A soft answer turns away wrath, but a harsh word stirs up anger" (Proverbs 15:1). Or by Paul, who wrote, "Let all bitterness, wrath, anger, clamor, and evil speaking be put away from you, with all malice" (Ephesians 4:31).

God Himself is the answer to the question of suffering. Why does suffering exist in the world? This is the critical question at the heart of Job's story. Yet, as we have seen, it is never answered—not even by God. Throughout Job, we are shown sources for suffering. Sometimes we experience tragedy because of Satan's attacks. Sometimes we suffer because we are being punished for our sin. Other times we suffer because God wants to catch our attention or because we are affected by the wicked choices of others.

In short, there is no universal cause *for* suffering. But there is a universal response *to* suffering. And that response is to trust in God. Job's story reveals that suffering and tragedy are real—yet they do not exist in a vacuum. We live in a universe created by a sovereign, wise, all-powerful God. We are connected to that God because He loves us and desires to be in relationship with us. Therefore, no matter what we experience in this life, we can leave the question of "why?" in His hands and simply trust that He is in control.

UNLEASHING THE TEXT

1) When have you felt most encouraged during this study? Why?

2) What are some unanswered questions you would like to have answered after completing this study?

3) In what ways do you relate to Job and his story?

4) How would you describe in your own words the answer to the major question of Job's book: *Why does suffering exist?*

PERSONAL RESPONSE

5) Have you rested in Christ for salvation? Explain.

6) In what areas of your life have you been most convicted during this study? What exact things will you do to address these convictions? Be specific.

_____

_____

_____

_____

_____

7) What have you learned about God's nature and character throughout this study? How should that knowledge affect your everyday life?

_____

_____

_____

_____

_____

8) In what areas do you hope to grow spiritually over the coming weeks and months? What steps will you need to take in order to achieve that growth?

_____

_____

_____

_____

_____

If you would like to continue in your study of the Old Testament, read the next title in this series: _Psalms: Hymns for God's People._

Also Available in the
John MacArthur Bible Study Series

The MacArthur Bible Studies provide intriguing examinations of the whole of Scripture. Each of the 35 guides (12 Old Testament and 19 New Testament) incorporates extensive commentary, detailed observations on overriding themes, and probing questions to help you study the Word of God.

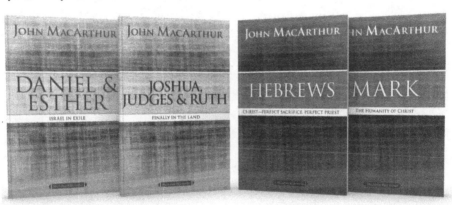

9780718033743	Genesis 1 to 11
9780718034566	Genesis 12 to 33
9780718034573	Genesis 34 to 50
9780718034702	Exodus and Numbers
9780310123743	Leviticus & Deuteronomy
9780718034719	Joshua, Judges, and Ruth
9780718034726	1 Samuel
9780718034740	2 Samuel
9780718034733	1 Kings 12 to 22
9780718034757	1 Kings 1 to 11, Proverbs, and Ecclesiastes
9780718034764	2 Kings
9780718034795	Ezra and Nehemiah
9780718034788	Daniel and Esther
9780310123767	Job
9780310123781	Psalms
9780310123804	Isaiah
9780718035013	Matthew
9780718035020	Mark

9780718035037	Luke
9780718035044	John
9780718035051	Acts
9780718035068	Romans
9780718035075	1 Corinthians
9780718035082	2 Corinthians
9780718035099	Galatians
9780718035105	Ephesians
9780718035112	Philippians
9780718035129	Colossians and Philemon
9780718035136	1 and 2 Thessalonians and Titus
9780718035143	1 and 2 Timothy
9780718035150	Hebrews
9780718035167	James
9780718035174	1 and 2 Peter
9780718035181	1, 2, 3 John and Jude
9780718035198	Revelation

Available now at your favorite bookstore.
More volumes coming soon.

THOMAS NELSON
Since 1798